8-26-58

BUSINESS PLANNING
FOR ECONOMIC STABILITY

Henry Thomassen

Public Affairs Press, Washington, D. C.

TO MY PARENTS

CONTENTS

1046798

PREFACE

Despite the encroachment of government, American business may yet reclaim economic stabilization as its own project. Warning flags for such a seizure have already been posted. This book is in response both to the centralists who oppose the move and to the "free enterprisists" who endorse it. It is an attempt to outline the chief implications of a business acceptance of the cycle problem.

The most challenging aspects of the firm's new role lie in the self-destructive nature of elemental rationality, in the choice of action in the face of uncertainty, and in the development of a general and genuine feeling of social responsibility. The associated difficulties far overshadow those of mere profit maximization. Nevertheless, at the risk of giving away the plot, I cannot resist announcing in advance that the work has a happy ending. Business and stability are finally united in an everlasting, many-sided ceremony which spreads joy (and income) throughout the nation.

The original manuscript from which this book has grown benefitted by the assistance of three members of the economics faculty of the University of Nebraska; they deserve my special thanks. Edward B. Schmidt offered reassuring enthusiasm for the project, Campbell R. McConnell provided thorough criticism of content and presentation, and Clarence E. McNeill so vigorously opposed the whole theme that I had no alternative but to speed its completion. In addition, I am particularly grateful to the editorial staff of Public Affairs Press for its generous constructive comments, patience, and understanding.

HENRY THOMASSEN

Newark, New Jersey

CHAPTER I

THE PROBLEM

An outstanding feature of contemporary United States' society is its genuine concern for the business cycle. Americans, more than ever before, are recession-conscious. Radio, television, and press daily picture an alert, even tense, people who watch constantly for stock-price downturns, who elect on the basis of fiscal-monetary platforms, who simultaneously acclaim and condemn "automatic stabilizers," and who, when unemployment looms as a real threat look to economists for advice they hardly dare accept. With respect to the latter, it is somewhat ironic that the business segment of the economy should be the last major element to pursue stabilization measures. Despite the relatively greater influence of the cycle on business profits, the initiative of government (the public) and of organized labor has preceded that of business, as is suggested by the Full Employment Act and recent guaranteed wage agitation.

It is not without significance that a cyclical control proposal is now originating in the business sphere. The emerging plan binds into an integrated whole those isolated elements of anti-recession practice which businessmen have been suggesting over the past ten or fifteen years. The "business proposal" is thus an explicit declaration of a lack of confidence in monetary and fiscal policy as means of controlling fluctuations in a capitalist system. Trust is placed instead upon general "business planning." "Government planning" may advantageously complement the programs of business to some degree. Nevertheless, the successful alleviation of the cycle depends upon a core of elemental business initiative rather than upon one of government.

The purpose of this study is to analyze and determine the principal economic implications of the proposed plan of anti-cyclical business policy in the American economy. It is, in essence, an attempt to uncover the details of operation inherent in what is here termed the "business planning proposal."

DEFINITIONS

The Business Planning Proposal. The term "business planning proposal" has reference to that unmatched cyclical control plan wherein "business planning" is generally practiced by the American business population. "Business planners" are thus thought of as the pro-ponents of such a scheme.

Business Planning. The term "business planning" is used herein to refer to that form of planning consciously undertaken by the existing independent business units of American society for the expressed purpose of moderating business fluctuations. In that it is directed toward aggregate stability, and further, in that it is enacted by indi-vidual, formally unassociated, business entities, this type of planning is unique. Clearly, it should not be confused with the frequently cited "business planning" proposals of Morris A. Copeland or Mordecai Ezekiel.[1]

Government Planning. The term "government planning" is herein used to denote that form of general aggregate economic planning by central governments as outlined in the United States Employment Act of 1946 and the British, Australian, and Canadian White Papers of 1945. It is based upon the theory that only the federal government acting in cooperation with industry, labor, agriculture, states and localities, and employing fiscal and monetary means can assure a con-tinuous level of aggregate spending commensurate with full employ-ment in a growing economy. Further, this planning implicitly and absolutely denies the socialist-type comprehensive master plan which designates the specific achievements demanded of the total economy and its constituents and which characterizes what is commonly labelled a "planned economy."

IMPORTANCE OF THE PROBLEM

Recessions (depressions) remain a real threat to the American economy. Despite the expanding role of our federal government in cyclical control, our nation continues periodically to suffer downturns in business activity, as evidenced in 1949 and 1954. Since efforts of the past few decades have proven less than completely successful in controlling recessions there would seem to be a clear-cut need for further investigation in this field.

Although any study in the area of counter-cyclical theory or policy can be deemed significant, it requires slightly more reflection to justify the study of one particular proposal. Especially is this true when one recalls the widespread support presently afforded the theory and policy of governmental fluctuation control. Still, it would be a grave error to assume that the governmental approach has been established as the only appropriate avenue of attack. It is the opinion of some leading economists and businessmen that, as Edward C. Simmons states, the positive role of the federal government in counter-cyclical policy involves its assumption of responsibilities far beyond its abilities to discharge them.[2] Nor does this overlook the fact that the very acceptance of these responsibilities may reduce their magnitude. However, businessmen, taking a practical outlook on the matter, increasingly point to the postwar period following the Employment Act of 1946 as a testing ground in which the accepted government measures proved inadequate. To economists and businessmen with this point of view, the study of some other means of cycle alleviation is essential.

One alternate gaining increasing favor in businessmen's commentaries is the one with which this study deals. Since this proposal has to date gone untried, one must find reasons other than achievement to account for its present popularity. Primarily, in that the business planning proposal conveniently "solves" the current real and/or imagined conflicts between the mitigation of cycles on the one hand and the avoidance of extreme centralism and economic stagnation on the other, the scheme attracts that bulk of United States' society which is sentimentally, if not concretely, bound to a "free enterprise" tradition. Secondly, the broad appeal of a new, basically "American" solution cannot be discounted. Finally, a plan which endorses the philosophy of many business groups to the effect that government interferences are largely accountable for the continued recession "abnormality" is guaranteed to gain much immediate, if irrational, support.

The recency of the businessman's attraction to this proposal is partially indicated by a comparison of editorials appearing in *Fortune* in the years 1938 and 1953 respectively. In June of 1938, *Fortune* wrote: "Every businessman who is not kidding himself knows that he does not know how to guarantee without government intervention, the markets with which alone his free competitive capitalism can function. Every businessman who is not kidding himself knows, that if left to its own devices, business would sooner or later run headlong into another 1930."[3]

Fifteen years later, treating the same general theme, *Fortune* commented that business heads had come to realize that they "can talk the country into depression" or into prosperity.[4] In fact, when threatened with depression, it now becomes appropriate to "Let business pursue . . . a 'readjustment' with vigour and determination, and the chances are overwhelming that the downturn will again [as in 1949] be so brief and slight as to be hardly noticeable . . . Indirect federal measures like those taken by the Federal Reserve Board to ease the money supply seem . . . appropriate to the current situation. Businessmen should be able to do the rest."[5] Clearly, the principal responsibility for anti-recession action is in thought, at least, being shifted to the business world.

A typical view of the "type of business men we need"[6] is exemplified in the person of Charles H. Percy of the Bell and Howell Company. In testimony before the House of Representatives Ways and Means Committee, Percy states that his first obligation "is not to protect my company but to serve the interests of the United States . . . first, we must do whatever is best in the national interest, and second, we must find a way that our company can adjust."[7]

Although speaking of tariff protection in this instance, Percy's attitude of social responsibility would presumably apply equally well to questions of stability. This viewpoint, says Herrymon Maurer, is typical of many of today's managers.[8] Like Ben Fairless of the United States Steel Company, executives generally recognize that, even in the face of recession, "the market is there, the money is there, and all in the world we [the businessmen] have to do is go out and get it."[9] These businessmen, too, no doubt support Ira Mosher of the National Association of Manufacturers in his contention that a full employment situation would be normal if the federal government could be relied upon to "properly" manage the money and credit system, to halt the granting and perpetuating of special privileges to economic groups, and to avoid the hindrance of private investment flows into job-making activities.[10]

That there is a significant tendency toward the development of a businessman who displays at least verbal loyalty to the concept of social responsibility is apparent; that the businessman is simultaneously charging himself with the prime responsibility for cycle mitigation is certainly implied.

More concerned with the potential of the latter than of the former is a statement appearing in a recent issue of the *Wall Street Journal*: "It cannot be stressed to often that modern long-range industrial planning is a tremendous factor in making the economic situation in the United States more stable than it has ever been before. Thirty years ago few corporations [like General Motors, Ford, and Chrysler] planned in this fashion."[11] In a later issue of the same publication, Joseph E. Evans, dealing with sales policy and economic stability, states that "the automobile manufacturers and dealers have to conspire to tame the American consumer and bring him into the captivity of orderly, regular, and predictable purchasing—not only as to volume and timing, but as between competing products. This is a truly awesome undertaking that might well give pause to the most agile advertising and promotion brains." [12]

The "awesome" characteristic of business planning relative to advertising and stability will become much more evident in later sections of this study. For the present it should simply be noted that the possible successes of business efforts in a stability program are today being considered in a new light.

In passing, it seems worthwhile to mention that the new outlook may perhaps be attributed in part to the stimulus of a recession-conscious labor group pressing for a guaranteed annual wage. As early as 1944 the United Steel Workers (CIO) made this demand of the basic steel industry. Since that time labor organizations have adopted the guarantee as one leading objective. Business, as represented by the National Association of Manufacturers, has by and large opposed the measure and has proposed as a more desirable substitute a program of "employment stabilization" based upon regularized production, and "sound" purchasing, merchandising, and research programs. [13]

The business reply to the labor demands is well portrayed in the following restatement of N.A.M. policy: "We feel that the whole problem of stabilizing production is one of great importance. For various reasons, individual companies may not be able to adopt plans guaranteeing employment. We, however, urge all employers to give careful consideration to this and any other methods of reducing fluctuations in production which have been successfully applied by many companies." [14] The fact that this policy was given verbal formulation before the formal labor demands of 1944 may somewhat undermine the causal sequence here suggested. However, and more significant for the purpose at hand, business thinking is becoming stability oriented.

Leading academic economists have been among those who have vigorously supported business planning. Walter P. Egle foresees a situation in which stability will emanate almost automatically from "an economy in which it has become rational for private business to counteract fluctuations with its own devices." [15] Wesley C. Mitchell long ago noted the import of individual efforts in solving the problem of adjusting supply to demand: "Combined with technical improvements is the day-by-day effort of every responsible businessman to follow current demand with vigilance, to take advantage of every favorable change, to guard against every decline, with all the skill which mother wit and practical experience can muster." [16] More recently, Hans F. Sennholz has commented that "booms and busts [are] . . . imposed upon us by 'omniscient' government economists and public officials who would like to do the planning for the citizens . . ."; he suggests that a withdrawal of government fiscal policy would do more to alleviate business fluctuations than the positive action is capable of ever doing. [17] Less extreme than that of Sennholz, and seemingly less near sighted, is a suggestion by Elmer C. Bratt. To him, a "dynamic price policy" focussing attention on the potential market and the long-run rather than on historical costs and the short-run offers a major weapon which businessmen may use to moderate the cycle. In the past, businessmen on the whole have given insufficient attention to the increase in demand which would occur with a dynamic price policy. [18] And finally, to summarize the views of the academic school of thought, Dexter M. Keezer states that business, by doing a better job of advanced planning, can do much to eliminate the drastic economic fluctuations which have been a feature of the American development. [19]

Similar viewpoints expressed by other businessmen and theorists could readily be cited. However, those indicated seem sufficient to show that although business planning is growing in terms of business and academic interest, it has to date escaped comprehensive analysis.

METHOD OF APPROACH

This interpretive study, based upon deductive, logical analysis, is divided into five parts. Initially, the implications of the business planning proposal for cycle theory are considered. Secondly, the implications for the business segment of the economy are treated. Here, the individual firm and its policies become subjects. In the third section, particular attention is focussed upon the organization which the plan imposes upon private business. The place of government within the framework is of concern in the fourth section. Finally, a summary and appraisal of the entire proposal is featured.

CHAPTER II

IMPLICATIONS FOR BUSINESS CYCLE THEORY

The assertion that business planning may solve the problem of economic fluctuations is an absolute denial of the belief, popular among many leading cycle theorists, that the capitalistic system is inherently or inevitably unstable. Further, the assertion is an implicit acceptance of the view that depressions are man-made acts, or, at worst, acts of God transmitted through man. In either case, man can provide his own cure. But, this cure is not to be found in a removal of government from the economic operations of the nation, as proposed by many recent naturalists. Neither does the remedy lie in the opposing and more popular policy of a planned introduction of compensatory government action. Moreover, the abolition of monopoly power in all its forms cannot be relied upon for success. For the proponents of the business proposal, the depressions of the past are directly attributable to inappropriate actions (reactions) by the businessmen of that day. The avoidance of boom and depression in the future therefore comes to depend upon right actions by this same social group.

As business cycles are neither inherent, inevitable, government-produced, nor monopoly-produced, so too they are not the guarantors of economic efficiency which some have maintained. That is, this business school of cycle control does not accept D. H. Robertson's verdict that recurrent depressions are the vital disciplining force necessary to produce a progressive advance in the effectiveness of labor and an overhaul in the methods of production and distribution.[1] Neither does this school maintain that stability and an optimum allocation of resources are necessarily coincident. Further, it does not agree with Alvin H. Hansen that economic flexibility and mobility are assured primarily through the periodic depressionary influence,[2] or again with D. H. Robertson and James A. Estey that fluctuations indicate and are the essential concomitants of progress.[3] The business planning proposal holds that appropriate action by businessmen can and should mitigate extreme fluctuations in our economy.

Business planning envisions the individual businessman as a

7

rational, informed being, capable of formulating and realizing his plans without the aid of a central coordinating agency. Here, implicitly, one finds an absolute rejection of the "dual morality of man" concept recently outlined by Karl Mannheim. According to the latter, man simultaneously exhibits two types of responses to right and wrong. On the level of general argument and insight, he will plead for the right thing, not in his particular interest, but in the interest of the community or nation in which he is included as a member. Acting in a given context, however, the individual will very often disavow what he proclaimed on the plane of generality. He is, as it were, "preaching water and drinking wine" as he reacts to the demands of society on two levels.[4] For business planning, it seems essential that the individual react for the common good, for economic stability, at either level of demand. At once it becomes clear that the institutions of the profit motive and the economic man must be severely modified if not abandoned entirely to allow the enactment of the program. Much more will be said concerning this subject in the next chapter. Here, it is important to notice only that the metaphysics of man takes on a new light in the business stabilizing scheme.

Although the philosophy of the business proposal superficially incorporates a wholly rational and pragmatic outlook, it might well be claimed that an element of mysticism is also introduced. Granting no central coordinating agency, it seems to follow that a power beyond the real economic world must somehow provide for a directed combination of individual plans leading toward the overall objective of economic stability. The power of rational thought might be proposed as the coordinating mechanism. However, no two men see any situation in an identical perspective or in the same degree of totality. Is one not then being extremely optimistic to assume that reason alone will lead men to "right" action? The point must be postponed for discussion in a subsequent section. However, its significance is immediately apparent. Even in this practical framework that denies natural order, there may still be a place for mystic guidance. Stephen Bailey's term, "serendipity," the twentieth century version of the invisible hand, may here be directly applicable.[5] And, whether the guiding force be rational thought or other regulating power, the coexistence of conscious stability planning and individual freedom rests upon its presence. Indeed, it is as a result of this super-power that elemental [6] planning can be considered effective in achieving a comprehensive objective.

Conclusion. This chapter has provided an overview of the chief implications of business planning for cycle theory. Even at this point, one significant conclusion emerges. The plan proposed demands individuals more able intellectually and more responsible socially than any envisioned by other current cyclical control proposals. The businessman must display a quality of foresight and of recognition seemingly as well developed as that of today's outstanding theorists. Beyond this, he must be able to relay his academic insights into practical techniques appropriate to his situation. He must be able to connect goal with action. The circumstances under which such achievements are most likely to be accomplished must now be uncovered.

CHAPTER III

THE RATIONALITY OF BUSINESS

Business planning implies that the problem of economic stability is mainly one of achieving rapid elemental adaptation to changes in particular circumstances. Hence, the ultimate decisions must be left to people who are familiar with these circumstances, who know directly of the relevant changes, and who recognize the resources available to meet them.[1]

It is at this point appropriate, therefore, to examine the business firm, its leadership, etc. In this consideration there is no need, initially, for distinguishing between the various market situations involved.

The Business Firm. The business firm is an entity that arises because of the division of labor and the fact of uncertainty. The former demands an integrating force which will organize, control, innovate and direct resources; the latter requires a unit willing to accept risk or to insure the doubtful and the timid by guaranteeing a specified income in return for an assignment of their resources.[2] The firm is then a system of relationships which comes into existence when the direction of factors is dependent upon an entrepreneur, the latter here regarded "as the personification of a 'firm' rather than a particular individual in a pair of trousers."[3] Further, to use John R. Commons' terminology, the firm has continuity of existence and is a "going concern."[4] It is an instrument for transforming the services of persons and things into completed products. But, the firm is more than a system, a concern, or an instrument. It is a distinct being with a unique collective will (or personality) existing apart from the people who comprise it. Because of this individuality, in fact, the business planning proponents are able to speak of rational action by the businessman, or as here described, by the firm.

Rational Action. Rationality in any action demands that the actor take cognizance of: (a) the time dimension of all alternative actions open to him and of their consequences; (b) the multitudinous consequences of each possible action; (c) his uncertainty concerning the various alternatives and their consequences; and (d) his own value

criteria and the likelihood of change therein.[5] Having so evaluated
the situation, the rational actor makes what to him is the "best"
choice. His subsequent action is thus set apart from irrational
moves based upon an ignorance (real or imagined) of the alternatives and outcomes involved, upon illogical deductions and predictions, upon erroneous applications of normative criteria, and upon
dismissals of known criteria, alternatives, and consequences.

Rationality, or rational action, on the part of the firm demands
that it make conscious and logical adaptations of means to coherent
ends. For business planning, the ends are those which lead to aggregate stability.

By its very nature, rationality demands the balancing of one possibility against another, or, in other words, the use of compromise and
relativity. To compare, in turn, requires a knowledge of relevant
factors and an understanding of a criteria for weighing them. Business rationality is therefore limited by the factors that determine the
knowledge and the values of the firm. An ethical as well as a factual
issue is in question. In the latter there can be only one "best" answer
for any number of firms each equipped with the same understanding
of the identical circumstances which they face. In the former, however, the "right" decision is always value-affected; that is, the occur-
rence of the action selected is not a matter of indifference to the firm
concerned. Consequently, the proponents of the business planning
proposal seem to suggest either that all business units are equipped
with the same system of *relevant* values, or that the objective element
is the dominating determinant in every decision.

The latter possibility is eliminated as soon as one recalls that the
business planners envisage a socially responsible business entity which
recognizes the societal implications of its decisions and considers the
social interest (in so far as is possible and reasonable) in arriving at
these decisions.[6] Hence, in the business world, a uniform set of relevant values is implied to exist so that all firms may make universally
"right" policy choices.

Firm Rationality. Even if one were to grant the described uniformity of values, the ability of the firm to reach a decision that logi-
cally joins means to ends from the standpoint of both the actor and
the observer (with a wider knowledge of the circumstances) would
not be established. Nor would observations of business practices provide much support for such a contention. Firm action in the past has
not demonstrated with significant frequency the unique characteristic

of rationality found in the presence of a time interval, a period of mental deliberation, between the formulation and execution of an action.[7]

By and large, the businessman is unable to carry in his mind a picture of a continuous variable.[8] That is, in the selection of the several and varied consequences that can be expected to arise from a particular action, attention will at once tend to become concentrated upon only the typical outcomes in imagined future situations, the first rule of simplification being that all variables must be reduced to a few discrete values. The number of typical outcomes depends in part upon the liveliness of the imagination in conjuring up alternative future situations and in part upon the time available for disturbing elements to enter in, that is, upon the image date. After a process of reduction, the firm is likely to be concerned with one or two typical outcomes, G. L. S. Shackle's *focus gain* and *focus loss*,[9] rather than with the entire distribution of potential possibilities. Consequently, general comparative analysis is wholly eliminated.

An even more stalwart barrier to rational action is the firm's inability to gain extensive knowledge of the circumstances it faces. In the present situation, firms perceive the setting before they react; but, as all human personalities, they react not to what they perceive but rather to what they infer. Moreover, it is a fundamental fact that man can survey (and hence infer from) only a limited field. Nor is it likely that any man will ever be able to see the needs of others as vividly as he sees his own, or to be as quick in his aid to the remote as to the immediate necessities. Yet, to act rationally, the firm must know not only the immediate consequences of its actions but also the distant, and indeed, the immediate and distant consequences of the actions of its associates. Small wonder then that Herbert A. Simon, after so viewing the gigantic task, concludes "... it is impossible for the behavior of a single isolated individual firm to reach any high degree of rationality."[10] The degree which is attained must depend upon the elements already mentioned and, in addition, upon the accuracy of the firm's expectations.

The Role of Expectations. Expectation refers to the act of creating imaginary situations, of associating them with named future dates, and of assigning to each of the hypotheses thus formed a place on a scale measuring the degree of one's belief that a specified course of action on one's own part will make this hypothesis come true. Expectation is the factor which gives a *going concern* its *raison d'etre*. The firm lives in the future and acts in the present; the will of the businessman acting today is projected toward tomorrow's results which then come to be expected.

The firm's evaluation of the attractiveness of future courses of conduct is hampered not only by its inability to view a continuous variable. More formidable is the fact that an essentially unique future event viewed in isolation defies prediction and the probability concept when applied in this instance is without meaning. As William Fellner describes the circumstance, "Entrepreneurs in their probability forecasts are throwing a given set of dice only on a single occasion. The previous throws were with different dice and the subsequent throws will be with still others. The dice are irregular and the entreprenuers can at best attempt to appraise the effect of the irregularities on the frequency distributions that would be obtained with the 'present dice' if they were thrown many times. In these circumstances the frequency distribution estimated for a hypothetical sequence of throws is no unique determinant of 'intelligent conduct.' "[11]

This being the case, the business scheme proponents could perhaps be thought of as agreeing with George J. Stigler that, despite the inapplicability of the probability concept, there is yet a way in which the single business firm can predict: "The prophet is an artist, not a scientist. And because his technique is an art, it cannot be formulated into generalizations which will permit others to forecast mechanically with precision." [12]

The Problem of Uncertainty. By now the reader will no doubt agree that in the face of uncertainty the actual execution of activity becomes in a real sense a secondary aspect of a firm's life. The primary problem is one of scanning the economic horizon and deciding what to do and how to do it. Moreover, the more rational the firm attempts to be, the further it must look into the future and there the more uncertain things appear. But, it is that uncertainty which cannot be measured by a probability coefficient that presents the prime challenge. The easiest and sometimes only way to deal with it is through irrational action. The firm is guided to select some act above another without knowing in quantitative or qualitative terms which consequences best contribute to the means-ends chain of objectives culminating in a given *summum bonum.* Action is based upon the *a priori* motivations of intuition, belief, or conscience, is directed by instincts and impulses with mystic or non-mystic origins, is molded by inertia and immobility, or finally, is guided by the subjective feelings of trust, fear or affectivity ranging all the way from sympathy to passion.[13]

While irrational action circumvents true uncertainty, the process of grouping and consolidation reduces it. Although on an elemental level uncertainty remains, in the aggregate and in large numbers, true uncertainty can be successfully transformed into a meaningful probability coefficient (Jevon's Law of Numbers). Clearly, however, this means is inapplicable for the individual firm concerned with single unique future events.

A system of information dissemination, including perhaps reaction functions for associate firms, might be postulated as a technique for treating true uncertainty. However, it can be of great significance only when employed in aggregate predictions. Each firm's decisions depend to some degree upon other's actual and anticipated conduct. Further, the elasticity of firm expectations varies. Hence, information as to typical reactions, present reactions, past reactions, and probable future reactions of associates, all aggregative measures in a time or number sense, cannot be relied upon to reduce elemental uncertainty to any important extent.

Probably the commonest and most erroneous means of treating immeasurable risk on an atomistic level is that outlined by John Maynard Keynes. It has become a convention, he maintains, to assume that the recent past will continue into the future.[14] William Fellner describes the same reaction as one in which psychology enters to translate past experience, derived from instances belonging in different universes, into terms of a hypothetical homogeneous universe consisting of many cases such as the (actually unique) case faced.[15] Fortunately, the fallacy of this approach has been widely recognized.

History does not accurately repeat itself. From an aggregative view in either time or number terms, the present may well exhibit an intimate link with the past. On the elemental plane too, the relationship may be intimate. But the point is that it need not be and in many cases will not be. If an aggregate prediction based on a large number of time points relative to a single homogeneous circumstance could be achieved, the uncertainty facing the individual firm would be much reduced. However, over time there simply is no such set of homogeneous circumstances from which to generalize. Thus, on the micro-level, and this is the only pertinent level for the business planning proposal, the predictive value of what has gone before is very often insignificant and irrelevant and is always uncertain.

A challenging and most promising method of treating elemental uncertainty has been suggested by George Katona. To him, expectations are not innate. Nor are they appropriately based on past experience (recent or distant) or on the frequency of past experience. Rather, a firm's expectations, to be accurate to any worthwhile practical degree, must rest upon an intelligence, an understanding, a comprehension of circumstances. There must be a realization that conditions change and that there is consequently a continual need for choosing new and more appropriate policies. Only when the firm can recognize the vital elements of any situation and see the essential relationship between those elements and its overall objectives will it be able to reduce uncertainty without appealing to the law of large numbers.[16] Only then, too, will the firm be in a position to select those alternatives which best fit into the means-ends chain terminating in aggregate economic stability.

It should be noted that uncertainty need not always introduce a new dimension into behavior. As Albert G. Hart comments, there are many things people do because of uncertainty which they would not do for any certainty whatsoever.[17] On the other hand, there are certain classes of data, which if known with certainty, would lead to the same action as each possible uncertain situation. Probable or expected values may inspire the same action as certain values. To use Jakob Marschak's illustration, "The effect of Hinduism on the packer's business is the same whether beef eating has or has not the consequences in future life which that philosophy asserts." [18] Nevertheless, uncertainty does on some, and probably on most, occasions lead to actions different from those that would result were the situation certain. Consequently, the business firm is still faced with the primary problem of uncertainty reduction. That the problem has not yet been solved is emphatically suggested by a brief review of authoritative opinions on the subject.

The Practical Treatment of Uncertainty. Before proceeding, it should be recognized that the presence of uncertainty does not preclude rational action any more than the presence of certainty guarantees it. As noted earlier, firms by and large do not display rationality. But their inability to reduce uncertainty is only one of the accountable factors. Uncertainty only sets the time and area limits within which behavior can be planned. Within these limits, that is, within the space of certainty or reducable uncertainty, rational action may or may not occur.

By and large, business enterprises fail to reduce the uncertainty facing them because they make no attempt to do so. It would appear that many firms depend upon a spontaneous urge to action without regard to the "outcome of a weighted average of quantitative benefits multiplied by the quantitative probabilities." [19]   Gerhard Colm contends that modern businessmen still rely largely on hunches of other people's behavior.[20]   Louis Baudin holds that business decisions are the outcomes of impressions, hopes, fears, and gambles of the future.[21] Speaking in the same vein, George Katona and James N. Morgan observe that decisions occur most frequently as quasi-automatic responses to particular circumstances or as habitual action.[22] Arthur C. Pigou asserts that sympathetic and epidemic excitement largely sway the commitments of individual firms.[23] In summary, one may safely say that for reasons of lack of knowledge, the pursuit of the easy and the enjoyable, sheer laziness, or other varied cause, firms tend to bypass rather than reduce uncertainty. Commonplace is the outlook contained in a recorded business leader's statement: "We are pressed for time this morning and must decide this matter at once. Tomorrow we can figure out the reasons."

Summary. The business firm must be rational if it is to fit into the business planning scheme of things. It must act consciously so that every action is a part of a means-ends chain culminating in aggregate economic stability. But, the "right" decision rather than the "right" action presents the firm with a major challenge. Businessmen have little experience in rational action. Their apparent inability to visualize a continuous variable, to gain an extensive knowledge of consequences, and to develop a uniform system of values relative to stability achievement stand out as barriers to meaningful activity. Of greater significance, however, is the limit imposed by uncertainty. In the past, expectations have been irrational for the most part. Too intimate a connection has been perceived between the future and the past or the future and the present. Blind action has been common. Seldom has the firm been educated to the degree that it was willing or able to analyze its circumstances, see the significant elements, reduce the uncertainty it faced, and proceed rationally. Nevertheless, it is just such a behavior process which is demanded.

MOTIVATION OF THE FIRM

The discussion thus far has proceeded without specific reference to the elements contained in the uniform set of values (motives) which the business planners imply influence the rational firm. These motives must now be considered.

The Profit Motive. If maximum profits can be made the *summum bonum* of a means-ends chain for firm behavior, and further, if such rational action in and of itself guarantees the attainment of aggregate economic stability, then one may justly say that business planning suggests the profit-maximization theory. Further, granting this to be true, if it should be shown that firms are in fact not motivated by the profits prospect, the stability proposal, for the present at least is considerably weakened. It becomes a thing of the future when firms have been educated so that they are capable of meaningful conduct. Putting first things first, it is appropriate to test for rationality in the "profit motive."

A word of caution is in order. To test the rationality of the profit motive is not in any sense to test the validity of the profit-maximization theory. The endeavor here is simply to determine if the behavior that ensues from the motive of profit-maximization is consistent with that demanded.

Armen A. Alchian and Gerard Tintner have convincingly outlined the nonsensical nature of profit-maximization.[25] Because rationality implies the existence of a well-ordered system of preferences (a means-ends chain), the selection of profit as the *ranking criterion* demands behavior which leads to profit maximization. However, faced with uncertainty and the inability to solve complex problems containing a host of variables even though the optimum is definable, any action by the firm will give rise to a distribution of potential outcomes (which are also overlapping) rather than to a single unique outcome. This results from the definition of uncertainty itself. Essentially then the firm must select the optimum distribution of potential outcomes since there is no such thing as a maximizing distribution, unless of course, one assumes that potential distributions are non-overlapping. In the case of the latter, one is dealing with a particular rather than the most general form of uncertainty. That a form of uncertainty which denies overlapping may exist is granted; that an overlapping variety more commonly prevails must also be obvious. Consequently, in that uncertainty yields no single-valued functions [26] of expectation, the profit-maximization construction becomes an "irrelevant tautology." [27] Only with certainty could such a function result.

Clearly, only the naive and the optimistic would suggest profit-maximization as a practical concept for the individual business firm. If the firm is to be rational, some other criterion must be adopted. The distribution of possible outcomes emerging with uncertainty forces the substitution of a multi-valued general preference function. Moreover, the business planning proposal gains strength by this substitution. By rejecting all single motives as prevailing behavior guides, the plan can operate with firms who achieve only a fair degree of uncertainty reduction and hence are only partially rational in their conduct. In this sense at least, the business planning proposal seems to be a practical measure.

Summary. In short, single-valued functions cannot serve as *ranking criteria* for the rational firm facing uncertainty. Although a quick review of works on the subject could depict a host of other values that might be substituted in a general function, that study will be left to the reader. The following chapter gives attention only to the multi-valued preference function implied by the business planning proposal.

CHAPTER IV

PREFERENCE FACTORS

Business planning implies a rational firm striving to realize an optimum preference function. The purpose of this chapter is to determine the specific objectives which will lead the firm to action productive of aggregate economic stability.

Aggregate Economic Stability. Economic stability, as the term is herein employed, demands general price level stability and full employment. The former denies any marked trends or sharp, short-term movements in general prices and at the same time allows for flexibility of individual prices. The latter refers to the condition in which qualified people who seek jobs at prevailing wage rates can find them without too much delay. Frictional unemployment in the amount of three or four percent is permissible and sets the limit for unemployment within a stable economy.

The Role of the Firm in Aggregate Stability. Were there general agreement as to the causes of economic instability or as to the areas or means of proper remedial activity, the place of the firm in stability achievement might be more easily determined. However, such is not the case. Even a hasty perusal of any recent textbook on the subject suggests almost as many theories of the business cycle as there are cycle theorists. It then becomes impossible for the firm to minister to the causes of flux. Instead, admitting that the real causes are not yet known with certainty, the firm must concentrate upon compensatory action. Here, the firm can find a greater degree of academic accord, though certainly not unanimity.

Despite the claim that more and more large firms are utilizing long-term capital budgets and are engaging in even longer term planning[1] it is important to recall that experience in the field of stability-oriented conduct is very limited. Traditionally, professional mores and public opinion have held the cycle to be something beyond the responsibility of management, a phenomenon to which the firm must adapt itself. The business planning proposal must change all this. Fundamentally, the preference function of the businessman must display a new attitude in which procedure is secondary to purpose. In the words of Joel Dean, going against the cycle will require courage, intelligence, and confidence.[2] It will demand an emphasis on action for the general good and the long-run rather than for the individual good and the short-run. Or, as a leading member of the National Association of Manufacturers suggests, it will demand that the manager be willing to go back over the record of his company to try to find out what caused the ups and downs in his business. If he finds that this was something which he can now change, he must make the change.[3] Stabilization is thus intimately merged with the problem of general moral progress and the degree of success which it is reasonable to expect depends directly upon the felt urgency on the part of the firms for appropriate action.

At this point it must be emphatically stated that the stabilization of one firm's operations is neither an essential cause or result of aggregate stability. Stability, in addition to its call for a stable price level and conditions of full employment, implies progress and growth. Progress in turn suggests change. Stability is therefore a dynamic concept and is wholly unattainable through the maintenance and perpetuation of present organizations, tasks, and outputs. The stability of the whole can rest only upon the compensatory instability of its component parts. As Melvin G. De Chazeau points out, "It is just not possible to achieve general economic stability *and* dynamic competition through stabilizing component parts. It is futile and misleading to parade such accomplishments of individual firms as evidence of what business can do to maintain high productive employment."[4] Moreover, as will be more fully treated later, stability in the case of one firm's operations may well mean instability for another or vice versa. Clearly then, business planning for stability is of a far different type than that which stabilizes the operations of an individual firm.

The stabilizing tools in the possession of the individual firm are now considered in the separate areas of forecasting, price and wage policy, sales policy, research and innovation, and inventory and investment policy.

FORECASTING

The firm must be able to forecast in order to determine those actions which are conducive to the achievement of aggregate stability. As noted earlier, however, the determination of future consequences is hampered by the fact of uncertainty. Were expectations certain, the economic horizon—that is, the length of time over which the firms plan their behavior—would be indeterminate. As soon as even reducable uncertainty is introduced, however, this indeterminateness disappears.

Because of the risk premium which must be added to (or subtracted from) any future purchase (or sale) price, the effective goods prices become too high (or low) to plan transactions beyond some certain date.[5] And, the more flexible factor and product prices, the more mobile the resources, the more dynamic the technology, the more varied government fiscal, monetary and regulatory policy, the greater is the reducable (and/or true) uncertainty facing an individual firm and the shorter is its economic horizon.

Of particular import is the effect of general rationality on any one firm's horizon. So long as firms cling to a "maximum profits" practice, or even to a "profits" pattern, the reaction of an associate firm to an anticipated or actual circumstance may be predicted with some degree of certainty. Irrationality may be consistent. As soon as rationality is expected of an associate firm, however, it becomes virtually impossible to predict future reactions. Even if uniform relevant value systems are assumed for all firms, it cannot be expected that each firm will see every circumstance in the same degree of totality or in the same perspective. With increasing education, the variations may well be decreased but certainly cannot be eliminated. Therefore, with increasing rationality on the part of associate and affecting units, the business firm comes to face an increasingly uncertain situation. Its rationality becomes limited by a shortened economic horizon. Ironically, rationality is then its own restrictor. When practiced generally within any area of the economy or within the whole economy, the process becomes suicidal.

Seen in this light, and realizing that the firm must always allow for the actions of other firms in its expectations, the importance of aggregate forecasting measures and of aggregate economic information is considerably reduced. Of course, the uncertainty of rational action is reducable by an application of Jevon's law of numbers. But, as pointed out earlier, such a reduction is of little value to a single firm concerned with a unique future event. Further, the day in which statistical indicators or simultaneous equations of linear programming can be made to serve the local businessman seems a long way off.

Similarly, the significance of various production, sales, and price indices must be questioned. The dissemination of such information must assist initially in reducing the uncertainty of the scene facing the individual firm. Subsequently, however, this information gives place to a greater range of general rational action and hence to a still wider range of uncertainty and eventually to a shortening of the economic horizon for each included unit.

One might contend that the development of "intention-to-spend" reports is a major contribution to the selection of firm policy appropriate to the business scheme. Nor may such reports be condemned simply because they do not always prove to be accurate. However, they must be decried because they are inconsistently and indeterminably accurate.[6] They involve an element of true uncertainty or a risk allowance so high that their contribution to stability planning may well be a negative one of shortening the firm's horizon. In the same way, published sales and output predictions of particular firms or industries may be of negligible value. Although in the aggregate, positive and negative variances of firm and industry estimates may counteract each other so as to yield a meaningful probability coefficient, for a single firm "throwing one set of dice on a single occasion" such estimates only add to the maze of uncertainty.

A final peculiarity of firm forecasting requires attention. If, as Kenneth E. Boulding expresses the circumstance, an astronomer foretells the movement of planets, that movement is quite unaffected by the fact that it has been foretold. However, if a firm forecasts a movement of prices, the fact that it made the forecast may itself affect the future of prices.[7] By making an announcement, however subject to inconsistent change, the firm sets in motion an influence of indeterminable magnitude and direction. For the aggregrate planners, the presence of such forces makes forecasting extremely valuable. Predictions may, in fact, serve to induce action that causes them not to be true or to be true. But, for the individual firm, unable to appeal to the law of large numbers, these reactions only cloud the scene. And, the longer the period over which the effects persist or are thought to persist, the more threatening and undirected the atmosphere becomes.

Conclusion. Since the announced intentions of firms create rather than destroy uncertainty, and further, since firms reflex as well as reflect on stated forecasts, the question arises as to the very possibility of forecasting on the elemental level. Perhaps, as Benjamin Caplan concludes, there is as yet no reliable method of foretelling which is invariant with respect to the forecaster.[8] A glance at the history of economic prediction reveals a mass of "successes" even though, in retrospect, many were based on the wrong reasons. Possibly then, for the single entity, prediction involves some mystic quality of intuition or insight. It becomes in essence an art where success depends upon the skill of the forecaster in viewing the whole situation and upon his flair for "feeling out" the fundamental movements. It becomes the application of the artist's touch to the statistician's skill. And, in the American economy which is to inaugurate the business planning proposal, the number of artists is large and the outcomes of their efforts varied. So seen, one may well agree with John H. G. Pierson that, "Forecasts are a precarious basis for stabilization programs." [9]

The firm of the business planning scheme, whatever its preference function, is by virtue of its fundamental inability to predict more than the immediate consequences of its action incapable of rationality to a very high degree. Consequently, the business planners must be relying upon some force other than rationality alone. Serendipity is perhaps the implied complementary power. More likely, however, it is the force of large numbers. That is, with a large number of firms, the probability of gaining aggregate economic stability approaches the arithmetic mean of the probabilities of individual firms acting in a manner favorable toward aggregate stability. Thus, firms should be rational in so far as is possible; however, their failure to achieve a high degree of rationality does not preclude the attainment of the stability objective.

FIRM PRICE AND WAGE POLICY

Although the firm's economic horizon is likely to be relatively short, some optimum preference function is nevertheless implied. An element of prime importance in this function concerns price and wage policy.

Flexibility and Elemental Planning. Just as an increase in the degree of rationality in the behavior of all firms reduces the potential of rationality for any one member of the group, so an augmented flexibility of the general price level must increase the uncertainty of the situation facing the individual firm. It's economic horizon must thereby be shortened.

Elemental Price Policy. As productivity within the firm increases, money wages may be increased while product prices are held constant. Such action would tend to maintain a stable price level, prevent the accumulation of excessive profits, and at the same time, allow a high level of receipts.

This policy is in basic harmony with the business proposal. Initially, a stable price level tends to be fostered. Secondly, this price policy suggests that firms need only the slight degree of profit intoxication offered by the lag in wage increases after productivity to induce them to perform; the profit motive is then not the sole or even the dominating influence.

In the third place, the price policy suggests that total spending is a prime determinant of the state of the economy. This is in no way a violation of the business proposal. Moreover, this price policy indicates that a high level of spending can best be maintained by distributing productivity gains in the form of wage payments rather than in profits.

Despite its general appropriateness for the business proposal, the described price policy is not without disadvantage. Beside the implicit assumption that the marginal propensity of the wage earner to spend profits is higher than that of the profits receiver, it is assumed that the marginal propensity of the wage earner is constant. This need not be true. Consequently, a new element of uncertainty is introduced into the circumstances facing the individual firm. Also uncertain in the view of any particular firm is the time lag occurring between realization of surplus by associate firms and the corresponding increase in money wages (incomes) that results. Both factors will act to limit the economic horizon of all firms and so to reduce the potentiality of rationality.

The last mentioned lag is important in one other respect. The longer and more certain the period, the greater is the likelihood of innovation and ensuing rising profits, rising wages, rising money incomes, increased spending (consumption and investment), and higher real incomes. The shorter and more uncertain the lag, the lesser the opportunity for economic progress, and because of a diminishing economic horizon, the smaller the opportunity for rational action. Finally, with the complete elimination of the time lag, that is, with the creation of perfect and instantaneous flexibility of wages, the greater the probability of the "functionless catastrophe" of which Joseph A. Schumpeter speaks.[10]

The "rising wage-constant price" plan seems to be at least one of the possible policies implied by the business planning proposal. However, as was the case in firm forecasting, this policy simultaneously acts to foster and limit rationality. It is only through the increased education and experience of the firm that the balance may be kept significantly positive.

Another alternative measure which might be suggested is the policy of dynamic pricing. It is a way of giving immediate attention through price changes to current effective demand; it is a practical policy for an economy in which price setting within varying limits is feasible. Simultaneously, it is a means of introducing an extreme amount of true uncertainty into the business situation. Its merits for the business proposal are thus severely limited and the scheme hardly needs further discussion here. Suffice it to say that individual firm analyses of changes in demand, both as to magnitude and direction, and of price adjustments required to meet them, are sources of much uncertainty. Add to this circumstance the indeterminateness of consumer reaction to the policies adopted and one sees the irreducable maze that surrounds the business unit.

Conclusion. Uncertainty looms so large in this area of firm choice that one price policy hardly seems preferable to another. Nevertheless, the firm must choose and act (probably act and choose is more realistic). However, because of the limited rationality possible in price action, stability can be expected to result only by virtue of a more certain element in the preference function or an omniscient power which takes over where rationality ends.

THE GUARANTEED ANNUAL WAGE

The prime merit of the guaranteed annual wage plan lies in the fact that it focusses attention on those stability measures which may be enacted on an elemental level. Simultaneously, it increases the optimum scale of firm operation. This increase, later to be deemed desirable, results directly from the increase in average fixed costs and indirectly from the imposition of a longer horizon upon the firm. The uncertainty of the latter may be expected to foster attempts at demand manipulation (meaning higher selling costs) and product diversification. In each case, firm growth is accelerated, and again, as shall be shown, the potential for rationality is increased.

Nevertheless, the guaranteed annual wage is a pseudo-stabilization scheme introducing an illusion and a rigidity that is inimical to business planning. In the long-run, despite any legislative acts that may be passed to the contrary, the firm can guarantee wages only to the extent that it is guaranteed the consumer demand for the product which it produces. No one has yet claimed to have stabilized buyer tastes or spending habits. In the short-run, although the regular payment of wages may aid in maintaining effective demand, the adverse effect of fixed commitments on investment can well result in aggregate production at a level too low to support the guarantee. The very existence of the guarantee may actually raise the propensity to consume. But, the propensity to consume products of the firm(s) offering the guarantee need not be affected. In brief, the wage plan in both short- and long-run provides no guarantee of either elemental or aggregate stability.

Although illusory in one sense, the guaranteed annual wage has very real consequences in another. The wage plan imposes a rigidity upon the conduct of individual firms which tends to interfere with their achievement of aggregate stability. From still another point of view, the wage plan imposes a pattern of rationality upon the firm. Its *summum bonum* is the maintenance of wage payments. Were this a rational step in the sequence of firm actions leading to stability, one could say that the guaranteed annual wage is implied by the business proposal. However, as indicated above, such is not the case. Hence, the conclusions relevant for this study may be simply stated.

The guaranteed annual wage plan is neither a substitute for nor a complement to the business planning proposal. Although the plan draws the firm's attention to the problem of business cycles and seasonality, it is as capable a destabilizing as a stabilizing force. More significantly, it imposes a pattern of behavior upon the firm irrespective of the contribution to aggregate stability.

FIRM SALES POLICY

The powers and limitations of marketing and advertising policy have received increasing attention in discussions of recession control during the past few years. Among more and more observers, there has been an implicit recognition that the economy is a stimulated economy and that advertising is a most economical means of contact.

However, firms have not used their sales policy to the best advantage either for the stability of their own operations or for the stability of the economy. Paul G. Hoffman, formerly of the Studebaker Corporation, describes the activity in this way: "We American businessmen have a strange sales habit. We cut our advertising and other sales expenditure when business is tough to get and we need it. Then we let those expenditures float sky high when business is easy to get and we have even too much of it. This is the exact reverse of sense." Moreover, this correlation between the trade cycle and advertising expenditures has intensified business fluctuations.

The Stability Potential of Sales Policy. Despite the conduct of advertising and marketing procedures in the past, there are still many who feel that this policy area has definite and significant anti-fluctuation potential. The potential of sales policy in cyclical mitigation lies primarily in terms of its effect upon demand. Thus, in order to keep spending levels high, firms may be able to diversify their markets, products, and means of distribution. Attempts to balance sales in each category in a compensatory pattern will then assist in maintaining income, ouput, and employment levels. Also, the timed introduction of new products so as to uphold effective demand offers much promise. Similarly, the implementation of techniques such as delayed billing, improved service and delivery, credit extension, and improved storage facilities, will no doubt contribute. Further, when the demand for a firm's product is in excess of its current output, a restriction of these same services will allow the firm to postpone the expansion of the plant and equipment and so contribute to a curtailment of the boom. Marketing plant and facilities can be improved in times when demand is weak or shows signs of weakening. Thereby, moreover, the firm will be in a better position to take care of greater sales when they are later realized. Such are the major possibilities. Their significance for business planning needs evaluation.

Sales Policy in Business Planning. Initially, the success of any sales policy is by no means certain. Buyers can be influenced, but only to a point, the point varying with time and circumstance. The consumer is a distinctly uncontrollable and unpredictable creature and particularly so in the purchase of products whose acquisition may be postponed.

Consequently, sales policies would seem to contribute best to aggregate stability if they are non-cyclical rather than counter-cyclical in nature. That is, the firm should adopt a policy in which promotion expenditures are increased whenever demand exceeds the output generated by a rationally planned firm investment program. This functional sales policy might advantageously be complemented by some amount of the previously considered dynamic pricing. That the economic horizon of the firm would be significantly shortened by the introduction of these two uncertain measures must be granted; that the law of large numbers might generate stability in such a situation must also be allowed.

A functional sales policy differs from a functional price policy in at least one significant aspect. While all sales promotion expenditures generate income and so assist in maintaining aggregate effective demand, all price reductions do not. The difference in outcomes occurs because of the factor of expectations. Price cuts may be taken to signal, and if Boulding's law of self-justification applies, *do* signal further price drops. Unless countered by other influences, therefore, price cuts induce pessimism and expenditure delays. In a similar period of decline, a functional sales policy involves increased expenditures, higher incomes, and if successful, the creation of an air of optimism. Ideally then, a strong effort at sales promotion should accompany any price decreases. Said otherwise, price and sales policies should be combined into a non-cyclical, functional firm program.

Conclusion. It is becoming increasingly clear that the success of the business planning proposal does not rest upon firm means-ends chains culminating in aggregate economic stability. Indeed, as has been indicated at this point, such chains may be impossible to formulate. However, non-cyclical planning geared to ends within the horizon of the firm creates the situation in which there is a significant probability of aggregate stability realization. The import of this statement will become more apparent as the argument proceeds.

FIRM RESEARCH AND INNOVATION

Closely related to the rational firm's price and sales policy discussed above, and to its inventory and investment policy yet to be considered, is its research and innovation program. Specifically, the considered introduction of new products suggests a prior directed plan of research and innovation. Further, it suggests the presence of a "shelf" of saleable products or practical innovations which stand ready for use whenever and in whatever market that price and sales policy fail to maintain demand. In such introduction, lies the essence of a growing stable economy.

The research program is an essential element of the firm of the business planning proposal. For its own survival and for the success of a functional sales policy, the firm's research and innovation program must be long-range relative to its output operations. So seen, planned research and innovation demand the foresight that is peculiar to the rational firm.

The place of an innovation program in the business planning proposal rests upon the belief that technological change stimulates aggregate demand. This widely accepted credence in turn rests upon the assumptions that technological change increases the demand for capital goods and/or that it raises the consumption function. In the case of the latter, new demands must emerge only at the partial expense of existing demands.

These statements demand qualification. "The discovery of new products and new methods," as Howard R. Bowen points out, "reduces or destroys the value of existing capital goods and creates a demand for new capital goods to replace the outmoded ones. But the conclusion that this increases the demand for capital must be provisional because obsolescence also exerts a deterrent effect upon investment." [12]   Said in other terms, technology restricts the economic horizon of the individual firm.   Obsolescence becomes a new risk factor for the rational firm.   To the extent that it is calculable, the risk can of course be allowed for by the adoption of new products of lesser durability, by higher interest payments on loans secured by capital, by smaller maintenance expenditures, and by other similar means. But, for the most part, the effect of technological change on obsolescence is truly uncertain and cannot be reduced to a probability coefficient.   Hence, the firm can rationally plan innovation for only a short interval.   And, paradoxically, the more firms (in the aggregate) that attempt to advance technologically, the shorter must the innovational planning period for each included firm become.   As before, rationality is its own saboteur.   It is vulnerable to a "gale of creative destruction" which, theoretically, can culminate in its own obliteration.

Nor are the effects of technological change limited to investment; the propensity to consume, too, is affected.   It is generally believed that technology boosts the consumption function by enlarging the range of products available to the consumer and by speeding obsolescence of existing consumer goods.   However, it is difficult to accept that spending is often (or ever) limited by a lack of objects to buy. With the exception of some dramatic innovations like the automobile or television which may have decreased saving, new demands are likely to emerge very largely at the expense of their existing counterparts.   Indeed, the expected rate of obsolescence may be increased so as to reduce the demand for one firm's restyled product.   Again too, the composition of demand may be shifted while its aggregate remains constant.   For the economy as a whole, the effect of technology changes is uncertain and may be one of lowering, raising, or leaving unaffected the average propensity to consume.   Similarly, the outcome of an innovation by a single firm must be recognized as uncertain in so far as both associate firms' and consumers' reactions are concerned.

Conclusion.   Because of the uncertainty that arises with technological advance and which is associated with the ensuing demand for capital and consumer goods and with the emergent form of competition, the single firm's economic horizon for research and innovation is relatively short.   But, to the degree that rationality is possible, the firm of the business planning proposal should complement price and sales policy in a non-cyclical behavior pattern.

If one accepts the prominence of inventory investment as an aggravating agent in minor cycles, then the preference function of the rational firm of the business planning proposal can be expected to indicate an appropriate inventory policy.

Proper inventory policy for a firm has long been said to consist of maintaining such a relation between output and shipments (or sales) as is required to support the normal functions of production and selling. But, as long as investment in inventories is bound to either sales or shipments by a rigid ratio, it can only serve to accentuate cycles in demand.

Using the theory of inventory cyclical influence as a guide, the individual firm of the business proposal should attempt to use inventories as a buffer which will minimize the fluctuations in its employment and output. Inventory investment, providing for a uniformity and a continuity in output operations, will then trace a cycle roughly inverse to that of sales, and the inventory-sales ratio will vary over the cycle of demand for the firm's product.

Planning, Inventories, and the Production Period. Given products with the same degree of perishability, convenience in storage, and cost of storage, the longer the lag between an increase in demand and the increase in output which results, the greater would seem the advantage of the buffer-inventory policy for the individual firm. However, the longer the demand-output lag, the greater the uncertainty of realizing augmented sales of the higher demand and, if this uncertainty is reducable, the greater the cost of maintaining inventories. This increase in costs is explained by the presence of a "change in mind" risk allowance and by similar allowances (if they can be made) for the risk of losing technical superiority.[13]

Summary. The ideal inventory policy for the firm planning for economic stability is in essence non-cyclical rather than counter cyclical. In that respect, the inventory policies are no different from those of price, sales, and innovation already treated. Further, inventory planning, as all planning, is limited by the economic horizon of the firm. This, in turn, is closely related to the duration of the firm's demand-output lag. In so far as the uncertainty concerning the effective demand that will exist at the time the output is released is not reducible, the firm's economic horizon is shortened and its inventory policy is confined.

INVESTMENT POLICY

As already indicated in Chapter II, investment is viewed by many, if not most, cycle theorists as the key factor in economic stability. A representative statement of this school of thought is provided by Melvin G. De Chazeau: "The heart of the cycle problem is in the instability of investment and if private business is to contribute to greater economic stability, it must make some progress toward greater regularization of its investment practices.[14] It is with the investment "regularization" policy of the individual firm that this section is concerned.

Private Functional Finance. Following the discussion in the preceding section, it might be felt that business can aid in maintaining aggregate stability by enacting a system of private functional finance. That is, surpluses which accrue when the demand for individual outputs is high are spent (primarily on plant and equipment) during periods when that demand is low. Unfortunately, this position cannot be upheld. Although in periods of weak demand for its product, a business enterprise may spend more than its current income, this spending most frequently has its source in disinvestment rather than in reserve funds. In so far as this is the case, businesses contribute to unemployment rather than to employment through a "functional" finance scheme.

Both the accumulation and the disposal of surpluses present severe problems for the firm. Initially, the creation of a reserve of idle cash funds in times of high demand for one's output is entirely foreign to business psychology. Most frequently, reserves are invested in inventories, receivables, plant and equipment. Thus, when the demand for a firm's product declines, the surpluses are available only after liquidation. In the case of inventories and receivables, this can no doubt be accomplished without extreme difficulty, although it will normally involve some loss. However, even when retrieved, these funds may not be wholly available for spending. The firm is geared to a high volume of production and must operate at a reasonable capacity to pay all of the factors employed. Therefore, though cash funds may be realized by liquidation in times of slack demand, a goodly portion of these funds must be held in readiness to start production at the first hint of profitable operation on an increased scale. Plant and equipment acquired in times of high product demand and hence representing surplus usually prove excessive in periods of decreased demand. Nevertheless, they too can be liquidated only with difficulty and only at prices below costs. To the extent that they are liquidated, disinvestment occurs, creating unemployment and a decline in the nation's effective demand.

The tenet that losses should be minimized in any period of activity has been firmly entrenched in the business community. Indeed, it seems unrealistic to attach more than minor importance to those operations which may have been conducted despite the excess of variable costs over revenues. It is true that, in so far as temporary losses are concerned, inventory liquidation frequently allows the firm to stay in the market. However, when revenues are inadequate to meet operating expenditures over an extended period of time, the investment of surplus in increased productive facilities precludes the effective operation of a system of elemental functional finance.

In brief, a system of elemental functional finance using profit revenues does not seem to be implied by the business planning proposal. Its rejection comes not because it is a destabilizing force—it is non-cyclical and random in nature—but rather because it is not a feasible measure. Another means of "regularization" must then be suggested.

Growth, Competition, and Investment Planning. Although elemental functional finance has been found non-practical, it must not be construed that elemental planning of investment has been simultaneously rejected. Within the limits of the economic horizon, investment planning which is determined by the growth prospects of the industry and the firm and the competitive position of the firm, rather than by the fear of economic collapse, remains to be considered. In that it fosters the random nature of component instability, this type of "regularization" seemingly fits within the framework of business planning.

Nor is this type of planning undermined by the varying lengths of the economic horizons. Instead, it is upon this variance that the stability of the business plan hinges. Although the very achievement of planned growth in some firms can only be purchased at the expense of other firms, it is the fact that some are failing while others are succeeding that gives the business stabilization scheme its potential. When all, or the majority, fail or succeed simultaneously the boom and depression of the traditional cycle result. And, when all plan relative to the cycle using prices as their sole guide, the cycle is inevitable. Therefore, it is the theme of this chapter and of this entire work that non-cyclical planning alone can produce that random variation which the business planners envision as a generator of aggregate economic stability.

The "regularization" of investment does not mean that the firm will provide uniform annual outlays in plant and equipment. Nor does it mean that the short-run will be neglected. It does mean, however, that projects adopted for long-run purposes will be executed as planned even though short-run markets decline. In addition, it implies a short-run flexibility and a willingness to make short- and long-run adjustments to variations in the length of the economic horizon. A more rapid readjustment and recovery of weakening firms while others are still strong can mean continuing high employment for the economy as a whole. In this readjustment, pursued on non-cyclical grounds, lies the alternative to the simultaneous and sequential failure, readjustment and recovery of the majority of the firms as has occurred in the past.

Incentives For Regularization of Investment. With respect to the incentives for the regularization of investment (and indeed of all aspects of firm policy), the business planners seem to put the attitude of social responsibility first. The firm might also be significantly influenced by the likelihood that the planned development of capital facilities will be more efficient than hurried impromptu efforts stemming from the pressures of current and urgent demand. Further, long-run investment may be encouraged in that it keeps attention focussed on the developing (or declining) markets, and hence gives recognition to opportunities before they occur. In addition, long-run planning coordinates the price, sales, innovation, and inventory policies into a single meaningful and harmonious movement. Such a movement is of particular merit under the influence of automation.

Automation. To most people automation means merely increased mechanization. In a stricter sense, however, automation is a methodology and not simply a matter of technology (except in the broad sense) or a replacement of human labor with machines. It is a projection into economics of a philosophy based upon the principles that economic activity is a process, that there is some order behind the seemingly random flux of economic activity, and that every process must contain some means of self-regulation.[15]

Under automation, production cannot, as it did in the traditional system, absorb the risk of economic fluctuations, or at least only to a very limited degree. Production must be continuous at a set level of output over some period of time, short-run adjustments being possible only at exorbitant costs. A first condition for automation is then the establishment of a predictable, stable, and expanding market for the firm. A firm's various price, sales, research, inventory and investment policies must be geared toward this end. They must allow for technological change and the systematic obsolescence of products and processes. They must work together in a manner that is organismic rather than mechanistic. Planning in a non-cyclical, growth-directed, market-based manner becomes an absolute necessity. Herein lies the essential coincidence with the business proposal.

Although few contest automation's demand for rationality, most question its ability to maintain employment, or as it is more frequently stated, to avoid the creation of unemployment. For the proponents of the business planning proposal, this quandary can hardly go untested.

Automation releases some men from some jobs. According to the traditional theory, there follows an automatic re-absorption of these technologically displaced workers. In the dynamic industry, cost per unit of ouput decreases, price decreases, and profits increase. If the elasticity of demand for the dynamic product is unity, there is no change of employment in the dynamic industry; if greater than unity, there will be an increase in employment in the dynamic industry; if less than unity, there will be unemployment in the dynamic industry but there will also be an increase of employment elsewhere because of the transfer of purchasing power which ensues from the lower prices and higher profits in the dynamic industry. Thus, technological unemployment is impossible.

Nathan Belfer has convincingly penetrated this position.[16] First, he grants, with the neo-classical school, that rigidities of various kinds upset the smooth process of absorption that is postulated. Secondly, he notes that the automatic reabsorption theory tacitly and erroneously assumes the same labor-output ratios to prevail in all industries. Therefore, although automation need not cause unemployment, it may very well do so. The relevant elasticities seem to be the determining factors.

Similarly, the degree of union management cooperation may have an impact on the "unemployment effect" of the automation process. Appropriate timing and rate of introduction of new productive functions will allow workers an interval for smooth readjustment to the new environment.

But, automation cannot be expected to permeate all branches of production. The lack of a standardized product, the need for personal services, space requirements, and the cost of equipment will limit its introduction into such lines as construction, agriculture, mining, retailing services and the professions. Perhaps, as Walter S. Buckingham concludes, automation will be limited to those industries which employ at the most twenty-five percent of the labor force.[17]

To the extent that automation appears in the American economy, it is from the business planning point of view very desirable. Primarily, it fosters rationality of a non-cyclical nature. It makes the adjustment of short-run circumstances to long-run ends absolutely necessary. It demands a regularization of investment. That it may have an "unemployment effect" is acknowledged; however, the most recent testimony suggests this will be minor indeed.

The Feasibility of Non-Cyclical Investment. Melvin G. De Chazeau has claimed that there are many firms for which non-cyclical outlay programs are not feasible.[18] Were this true, the business planning proposal's potential would indeed be reduced. However, the statement seems clearly false. Every firm has some economic horizon, however short, and in accord with its motivations can rationally select its preference function containing congruous elements of price, wage, innovation, research, marketing, advertising, inventory, and investment policy. Hence, if there is a firm, there is an opportunity for non-cyclical policy. Moreover, it is an opportunity that demands no aggregate committees or agreements, administrative or legislative delays, or the subordination of a single firm to national or industry programs.

Summary. The business planning proposal implies that the rational firm will exhibit an investment policy which is regularized with respect to the growth and market conditions for the industry in which the firm is included and for the firm itself. This policy, therefore, will be compatible with the non-cyclical price, sales, innovation, research, and inventory policies of the business unit. Private functional finance plans on an elemental scale are for the most part impractical. Hence, regularization must be achieved through other means. In this achievement the influence of a feeling of social responsibility on the part of the firm is primary. Of increasing influence is the role of automation. The latter lends itself to the business planning proposal in that it forces a long-range non-cyclical outlook upon participating units. Its promotion, to the extent possible, would therefore help the elemental pursuit of stability.

CHAPTER V

THE ORGANIZATION OF INDUSTRY

In the consideration of the general preference function, firms have been treated as though each existed within the same industry structure. The purpose of this chapter is to indicate the implications of the business planning proposal for the organization of industry, and indeed, vice versa.

The Relation of Size to Rationality. A condition of complete monopoly is certainly stable. However, this circumstance, socialistic or fascistic as one chooses, is alien to the concept of business planning as defined. Nevertheless, it soon becomes clear that the larger the firms in the economy, *ceteris paribus*, the greater the degree of rationality which can be realized by each.

Initially, large firms tend to place far greater emphasis on long-run planning than do small firms. Their frequent use of long-term capital budgets is a case in point. Moreover, in that the decisions of large firms are for the most part group determined, their policies tend to be more stable. A group provides the individual with a defense against outside pressures at the same time as it exerts a pressure toward intragroup conformity upon him. Further, the large firm uses a formalized decision-making process and a long chain of communication, both of which contribute to the inflexibility of behavior. As E. A. G. Robinson neatly states the point: "The big firm is a series of wheels within wheels, an elaborate hierarchy, in which every decision requires the consulting of the man, the referring him to that man, the permission of a third, the agreement of a fourth, so the decisions become endlessly delayed."[1] Too, the larger the firm, the stronger will be its external and internal financial positions. Similarly, the more accurate will it probably be in the anticipation of its capital outlays. Because the large firm has many separate investment projects, the discrepancies between its anticipations and its expenditures are likely to be random in nature and self-cancelling to some degree. Exigency blanket allowances can provide for the "unexpected" in a phase of planning not possible for the small firm.

From the foregoing, it follows that the economic horizon of the firm is extended as its size increases. Its potential for rationality is simultaneously augmented. And, since the economic horizon of any firm includes the actions of associate firms within its sphere of influence, an increase in the size of these associate firms further extends the first firm's horizon. At the same time, the period over which each of the associate firms can plan is augmented. Apparently then, the firm rationality which the business planning proposal demands can be infinitely enhanced by the growth of firms in the economy.

Significantly too, since the trend toward bigness (variously measured) in the American economy is unmistakable, the business planners seem to be incorporating and building upon an existing tendency.

Planning and Monopoly. Although the business proposal gains strength from the presence of business concentration, it should not be construed immediately that monopoly is of similar benefit.

Monopoly is always a matter of degree. It arises because of the imperfect substitutability of one product, service, or technique for another. And, substitutability, too, is always a matter of degree. That is, in the last analysis, every good or service is a substitute, however poor, for every other good or service. Consequently, monopoly is not only an implication of the business planning proposal—it is a fact of the prevailing economic structure. The question of significance thus becomes one of determining whether or not the business planning scheme which implies the existence of an increasing number of large firms also implies the existence of an *increasing* degree of monopoly.

Monopoly and Growth of Firms. There is no need here to discuss at length the many factors which have been put forth to account for firm growth. Suffice it to notice that as influential as the principles of multiples, of bulk transactions, and of massed reserves may appear to "free enterprise" extremists, many maintain that such incentives are largely insignificant. Potential competition and substitution so flatten the long-run cost and demand curves that there is typically no "optimum size" firm in any industry. Rather, there is a wide range of optimum sizes within which most firms fall. Thus, economies of size are probably much less significant than is generally believed.

The determinant of firm growth most frequently put forth by leading authorities today involves the acquisition of monopoly power. Joan Robinson speaks for the group when she says, "Given time to accumulate capital out of profits and acquire know-how and trade connections, there seems to be no limit to the ultimate size of the firm until a condition of oligopoly is reached in each of the markets for the commodities supplied by the industry, so that the last stages of the competitive struggle are too costly to be fought out." [2] The most pervasive and persistent influence on firm expansion is the quest for power to eliminate competition and to control the market. Empire-building rules over technology.

The Advantages of Monopoly-Inspired Concentration. Before one condemns the form of concentration which is aimed at monopoly purposes (or results in monopoly), it should be noticed that, despite avowed disadvantages, there are several significant claims in its favor.

Thorstein Veblen ably expresses one such advantage in the following terms: "In great measure the saving effected is a saving of the costs of business management and of the competitive costs of marketing products and services, rather than a saving in the prime costs of production . . . The amount of 'business' that has to be transacted per unit of product is much greater where the various related industrial processes are managed severally than where several of them are brought under one business management . . . The greater the parcelment of ownership, the greater the amount of business work that has to be done in connection with a given output of goods and services . . . It is in doing away with unnecessary business transactions and industrially futile manoeuvering on the part of the independent firms that the promoter of combinations finds his most telling opportunity". [3]

A second advantage grows out of the belief that technological progress depends upon a field as open as possible to the formation of new monopolies which help to curb and destroy old ones. Monopoly is thus a powerful engine of progress, far superior in efficiency to perfect competition. As Edward H. Chamberlin describes the complex circumstance, "How can anyone doubt that if a product or variation of a product, or a new and more efficient technique of production, could be instantly imitated by others, the incentive to make it would for most people be lost?" [4] And who can doubt that large-scale production would never be realized if competition could not be suspended temporarily?

In brief, the business planning proposal cannot be condemned simply because it implies concentration which aims at the securement of monopoly power.

Business Planning and the Self-Limiting Nature of Concentration. Joan Robinson has indicated that concentration which is pursued on monopolistic grounds eventually becomes too costly "to be fought out." [5] Moreover, as the degree of imperfection within the economy increases, the limits imposed by this "excessive cost" are approached earlier in the pursuit. In addition to the pure economies of scale, the established monopolist's position is bolstered and enhanced (and that of potential rivals is simultaneously undermined) by its favored capacity to gain investment funds, by the ignorance of the purchasers of its products, and by any monopsonistic powers which it may have acquired in the factor markets. Further, by virtue of its realized economic surplus (monopoly-monopsony profits), the monopolist is able to reduce price drastically for a period long enough to discourage potential entrants. Even more significantly, the Galbraithian principle of countervailing power, though insisting that monopoly begets monopoly, also indicates that monopoly limits monopoly. To the degree that monopoly is characteristic of concentration, concentration thus limits further concentration.

To summarize, the effectiveness of the business planning proposal increases with the increasing concentration of business which extends the economic horizon of the surviving firms. To the degree that such concentration is monopoly inspired and monopoly achieving, however, increasing concentration acts to limit further concentration. Rationality is once again its own saboteur. Hence, only when the economy is governed by a single monopoly can firm rationality and business planning gain full realization.

Business Planning and Oligopoly. Concentration alone may be judged to increase the potential for rational action within the economy. To the degree that oligopoly results, this potential is further increased.

The element of price rigidity characteristic of oligopoly extends the economic horizon of all firms affected by actions of oligopolistic units. This is not to deny that in the case of a few sellers acting independently, there remains an element of uncertainty, among others, as to the degree of intelligence and farsightedness of rivals and as to how promptly and in what manner rivals will rationally react to any move. Under these circumstances, "no assumption as to the intelligence which sellers apply to the pursuit of their maximum gain, short of omniscience, would render the outcome determinate." [6] Yet, the fixing of prices will surely contribute to such determinacy.

At the same time, unfortunately, price rigidity destroys the price feature of a non-cyclical firm policy. Further, price rigidity, it is alleged, is only one overt expression of a general inertia that accompanies oligopolistic concentration. To the extent that such allegations are true, the business planning proposal, which demands an alert, socially responsible, rational firm, irrespective of firm size, must be significantly weakened.

Investment and Concentration. Probably of greatest importance for the business planning proposal is the implication which increasing concentration holds for a pattern of non-cyclical investment. The reduction of uncertainty through elemental compensation plus the stability factors inherent in a large firm and in an oligopolistic market, allow an adjustment of investment to the long-run growth pattern envisaged for the firm and the industry in which it is included. The larger the firm, the greater the opportunity for the regularization of investment in accord with the long-run plan of rational action which the firm has selected. Too, the smaller the relative volume of investment in inventories that will be required to realize the plan.

Since investment is considered the key to cycle mitigation by many leading cycle theorists, the business planning proposal which implies an increasingly larger firm and an increasing stability of intra and inter-firm investment must be judged as a potential means of fluctuation control. In fact, it is largely because of this implication that the business planning proposal gains practicality.

Conclusion. This chapter has uncovered the implications of the business planning proposal for the organization of industry. In that the length of the firm's economic horizon increases with the size of the firm, the potential of business planning grows with increasing business concentration. Because the United States' economy exhibits a tendency toward greater "bigness", the business planning proponents are building upon a real phenomenon. Nevertheless, non-monopolistic concentration faces the limits of technological economies of scale and monopolistically-inspired combination yields an inherent restricting force. Thus, the rationality of the firm which is extended by increasing concentration is eventually limited by the same force which created it.

CHAPTER VI

THE ROLE OF GOVERNMENT

The implications of business planning for the firm, the industry, and the private economy in general having been indicated, let us now consider the implications for government.

Micro Versus Macro Planning. In that the business proposal explicitly denies the need for and the potential of aggregate planning, it is at once clear that the role of fiscal and monetary policy must be minor. Government would seem best able to contribute to economic stability by following a policy which aided the business units of the private economy in their non-cyclical operations. Spending to "bolster" particular areas of the economy or the economy as a whole is assumedly no longer necessary. Socially responsible firms acting in accord with their own growth prospects will, in combination, maintain spending levels. Government outlays must serve only to provide for government goods and services. Thus, the annually balanced budget becomes a more justifiable reality. Said in other terms, the business planning proposal implies a non-cyclical policy of government expenditures.

Monetary-Fiscal Policy. Certainly the monetary policy associated with compensatory spending and taxing or designed to substitute for such fiscal policy disappears when government actions become non-cyclical in nature. The government is no longer a balance wheel, so to speak, offsetting fluctuations in the private sector. Still it must provide for important community services and for basic development projects which underlie and support private industry. In accord with Alvin H. Hansen's theory, the appropriate monetary policy under the business planning proposal is thus one which is flexible enough to yield a money supply over the long-run commensurate with the economy's growth potentialities. Such an adequate money supply is a necessary, though certainly not a sufficient condition, for economic expansion.[1]

The Dissemination of Information. Since government can avail itself of the most highly trained forecasters, of the most effective aggregative and elemental techniques, and of extensive information on both the micro and macro levels, it is reasonable to assume that it can do much to reduce the uncertainty facing the firm. This does not deny that the concentrated firm using similar techniques can do much to help itself. However, it must be remembered that extended information, while lengthening the economic horizon on the one hand, simultaneously limits that horizon on the other whenever the actions of one firm depend upon the actions of its associates. In the purely competitive (and ever non-existent) model, information dissemination will act to increase rationality; in the real economy featuring varying degrees of monopoly, such dissemination may on balance produce no such result. As stated earlier (Chapter III), rationality is self-limiting in this situation.

The government powers of aggregate forecasting would seem to aid non-cyclical policy in direct proportion to the concentration of business. That is, the more concentrated an industry and the economy in general, the greater the degree of certainty which the provision of information will produce. It is true that business dispersion subjects business actions to the law of large numbers and thus serves to make "rationality-induced uncertainty" reducible. But, to restate a prior conclusion, such reduction is for the aggregate alone and in no way applies to the unique and single situation facing some particular firm. The firm depends upon the peculiar action of a rival (s) in any particular policy selection and the laws of probability are here inapplicable. Of course, the more concentrated the economy, the smaller the degree of irreducible uncertainty that arises because of such interdependence.

Regulatory Policy. In the area of regulatory policy, a legislative overhaul of the anti-trust laws seems to be implied by the business planning proposal. Since concentration furthers the rationality which leads to economic stability, the case for indiscriminate trust-breaking diminishes. But, in view of the fact that oligopoly has long escaped the restrictions of anti-trust laws, the withdrawal of this legislation is likely to have a much smaller impact upon the organization of industry than is superficially suggested. Indeed, as John K. Galbraith has stated, ". . . for most Americans, free competition, so called, has long been a political rather than an economic concept." [2]

As the business planning proposal implies an increasing concentration of business, so it appears to imply a greater influence of the business firm on the public at large. Business ". . . goes political as rapidly as it masses power." [3] Concentration allows the mobilization of financial resources and of the instruments for controlling public opinion. Thus, with the growth of firms, popular government becomes government by pressure groups and legislation tends to serve special interests rather than the common good. In this vein, echoing the early Veblenian utterances, John K. Galbraith speaks of the American as one controlled, livelihood and soul, by the large corporation.[4]

Essentially, consolidated organizations like the General Motors Corporation, the United States Steel Corporation, and the Standard Oil Company (New Jersey), each with stockholders and employees numbering in the hundreds of thousands and customers in the millions, exercise an increasing coercive power directly on those individuals within their respective domains and indirectly on the populace at large through their influence on local, state, and national legislatures. Businesses become virtual governments in themselves.

Although the deterrents to business concentration are largely withdrawn in the scheme of business stabilization, the need for government control of monopolies does not disappear entirely. Only the most extreme advocates of the plan would be inclined to accept that the firm will become socially responsible enough to operate without some checks. Private revenues and costs and the immediate situation are likely to take precedence over social costs and revenues and the distant situation in many business decisions. Nevertheless, powerful institutional checks inherent in the situation of monopolistic concentration itself seem to make the task for government relatively minor.

One form of check already mentioned is that of countervailing power. Chain stores and mail order houses have arisen to counter the original market power of strong suppliers. Unions oppose and check giants like United States Steel. Monopoly begets its own restrictions.

A second control influence which would take on greater import with increasing business concentration is that of potential innovation. Joseph A. Schumpeter has stated the case emphatically. "It is not . . . traditional . . . competition which counts but the competition from the new commodity, the new technology, the new source of supply, the new type of organization (the largest-scale unit of control for instance)—competition which commands a decisive cost or quality advantage and which strikes not at the margins of the profits and outputs of the existing firms but at their foundations and their very lives. This kind of competition is as much more effective than the other as a bombardment is in comparison with forcing a door."[5]

Moreover, this form of competition ". . . disciplines before it attacks. The businessman feels himself to be in a competitive situation even if he is alone in his field or if, though not alone, he holds a position such that the investigating government experts fail to see effective competition between him and other firms in the same or a neighboring field." [6]   Clearly, the Schumpeterian damper will be more effective the more difficult it becomes to maintain monopoly through patent and legal privilege.   Herein, therefore, lies one significant area for government action.

The Institutionalist Bent.   Sound business planning suggests the need for a reconsideration of business firm behavior.   Current price theory is unable to account for the actions of controlling industrial giants.   Nor is there any reason why it should.   Indeed, "Every scheme of institutions has an implicit logic of its own and it is no less important to know what the logic is than to know how the institutions came into being and what they are becoming." [7]

Under business planning profits are no longer the sole initiator or even the prime regulator of business activity.   Rationality and social responsibility are, through the process of concentration, encroaching upon former profit territory.   Thus, a new form of collective action— the huge corporation—must be analyzed and understood in terms of the concomitant social fabric.   The economy must be viewed from an institutionalist bent.   Only then can the role of government, interpreted in the broad sense which includes "business rule," be fully comprehended.

CHAPTER VII

SUMMARY AND APPRAISAL

It is impossible for any one of a large number of independent small firms, even when equipped with the best forecasting techniques and most extensive market information available, to foresee accurately the influence of its actions upon the aggregate economy. Because of the limited economic horizon, it is then meaningless in this instance to speak of rational firm behavior directed toward an end of aggregate economic stability. The firm can be rational only insofar as it reaches for goals which can be specifically related in a means-ends chain to some particular action. As the perception varies with the viewer, so the actions contemplated as productive of any selected end will vary. The business planning proposal in demanding a rational firm for its enactment must not then be thought of as imposing any particular fixed pattern of rationality on business elements. Rather, it ought to be recognized as a scheme that takes account of the differing lengths of economic horizons and allows for a random distribution of outcomes.

The Law of Large Numbers. Although numerous and small business entities are incapable of separately "planning for stability," from an aggregate point of view their actions may contribute to this overall goal. Given the institutional arrangement in the economy at any time (t), (m) of the existing (n) firms can be expected to act in a manner favorable toward the selected end. Said otherwise, (m/n) is the probability that economic stability will result from the individual and independent actions. Further, the probability of the Bernoulli inequality, where (p_i) is the probability of the action of any firm (n_i) being the "right" action and where (e) > 0 (no matter how small), can be made to approach one (certainty) as nearly as one desires by taking a sufficiently large value for (n). That is,

$$m/n \left\{ \left[\frac{P_1 + P_2 + P_3 + \ldots + P_n}{n} \right] \right\} < e.$$

The "success ratio" of achieving stability in the aggregate approaches the mean value of the "success probabilities" for the individual units. Clearly, the greater the probability of success in elements, the greater the ratio for the whole. And, the larger the (n), the higher the probability of the Bernoulli inequality.

The Necessity of Non-Cylical Planning. If the firm cannot pursue economic stability directly, it must contribute to the overall goal by following an indirect route which, *en masse,* and because of the law of large numbers, will result in the desired end. The probability that any business unit will act in a favorable manner clearly increases as its disregard for cyclical expectations increases. That is, a firm following a non-cyclical pattern of behavior has a higher success probability (p_1) than one which guides its actions by anticipated cyclical changes. This does not suggest that the probability of right action in the case of the single firm is high; it only suggests that the probability will be higher than if firms are guided by an expected business cycle.

The Desirability of Increasing Business Concentration. The probability of firm action conducive to aggregate stability increases as the economic horizon is extended. When this horizon comes to include stability itself (although at first and under oligopoly with a high degree of uncertainty), business planning can be directed toward the aggregate rather than toward non-cyclical goals alone. And, as the relation between actions and economic stability becomes more certain, the probability of "right" action by any business entity increases. As success probabilities increase, the mean value of such ratios increases correspondingly. At the same time, however, since an extended horizon comes about primarily through a concentration of business, the number of firms (n) decreases. Thus, the probability of the Bernoulli inequality must decline if only slightly. For the increased certainty of appropriate elemental actions, one must admit of a decreased certainty that such actions will raise the stability "success ratio" for the economy as a whole. That the latter outweighs the former, of course, does not follow.

It should be noted that the extension of the firm's economic horizon through increasing concentration occurs, in the main, because of a reduction in the uncertainty (formerly true uncertainty) concerning associate's behavior. Therefore, it is conceivable that firm cooperation could produce a similar extension. However, it appears that this could be achieved only at the cost of elemental freedom of action. Such being the case, one of the prime merits of business planning — the maintenance of firm initiative—would at once disappear.

Under business planning aggregate stability could certainly be guaranteed only as a condition of monopoly was approached such that the relative frequency of (m) with respect to (n) could be made to approach unity. But, there is no suggestion in the proposal that a fascistic (socialistic) economy is the desired goal. Rather, the emphasis upon independent action indicates that a condition of high business concentration coupled with some degree of uncertainty concerning stability achievement is to be preferred. That is, an optimum balance between concentration and freedom of firm action, though not defined, is implied to exist.

The Non-Cyclical Role of Government. Business planning bases its potential success upon the rational action of individual, formally unassociated business units. Consequently, there is no requirement for a counter-cyclical government policy. Spending presumably will be for goods and services to meet social commitments alone. Given wise administrators, the money supply will be governed by what the best authorities in the field deem a rate of increase adequate for some anticipated rate of growth in aggregate real output. (The challenge here is no more or less formidable than it would be under any other stabilization program or than it is in the current American situation.) Monetary policy in the popular "anti-cyclical" connotation will assumedly disappear. Regulatory and tax legislation allegedly will be revised so as to allow for the increasing concentration of firms. The collection and dissemination of market information of all kinds and concerning all areas may be expected to gain prominence as government's contribution to the extension of the firm's economic horizon and hence to economic stability.

The Basic Responsibility of the Firm. The responsibility for aggregate stability rests squarely upon the willingness of elements to enact a non-cyclical and/or stability oriented pattern of behavior. As long as monopolistic competition dominates the scene, firms must strive for stability through the indirect means of a non-cyclical program. Only when concentration (and oligopoly) extends the economic horizon to include aggregate stability can a business unit adjust its actions to favor the direct achievement of the overall goal. But, in this instance, as in that from which it evolved, the firm must use its own initiative to achieve appropriate action.

Special notice should be taken of the role of education and knowledge as it relates to the firm in the stabilizing proposal. Education in general and knowledge of markets and of the economy itself in particular, serve to extend the economic horizon of the business unit. An "educated firm" employing market information disseminated by government and associate firms will be able to trace the effects of its actions to aggregate stability better than the uneducated and uninformed. In terms of the Bernoulli inequality, the (p$_i$) can then be made to increase without concentration and the (m/n) ratio can be made higher without any offsetting effect from a decline in (n). The stability of the economy can be made more certain without destroying the system of a large number of independent firms. Again, however, even the educated and the informed will aid the aggregate cause only to the degree that they feel responsible for such actions as are possible within the limits of their horizons. In sound business planning, the independent firm rules.

As pointed out earlier, few students of business and/or economics have addressed themselves directly to the form of business planning herein considered. In the majority of cases, comments on "business planning" concern industry planning of the Ezekiel type. That this is a type of "business planning" is not denied. Still, it cannot be stated too emphatically that such programs should in no way be confused with the approach herein considered.

THE OPTIMISTS

Although the avenue which he would employ to achieve the end differs from the one put forth here, Walter P. Egle looks forward to the eventual success of a privately and independently insured aggregate stability. The burden resting on government initially will be shifted to the private units of the economy as these units gain confidence that stability will be maintained and that it is actually within reach.[1] Though somewhat less optimistic in his appraisal, Edgar M. Hoover has commented that the success possibilities depend largely on whether uncertainty can be reduced and whether the evaluation of uncertainty can be made more rational.[2] The point in question is the one extensively treated in the foregoing chapters.

Joel Dean states that there are some possibilities in the sort of program based upon action directed to ends other than maximum profits. However, these possibilities have seldom been realized in the past.[3] His limited support is echoed by David McCord Wright, when he says that "The degree of regularization which business self-planning can attain . . . will be insufficient to *avoid* the business cycle."[4] In the same tone, Irwin Friend and A. D. H. Kaplan maintain that the contribution of business planning to stability, though modest, is nevertheless highly desirable.[5]

Much more enthusiastic support is manifested by business leaders and groups. Harlow H. Curtice, for example, attributes the 1954 recovery to self-initiated business efforts; he believes that American industry "has the capacity and leadership to keep the economy strong and virile."[6] Seemingly by way of endorsement, the United States Chamber of Commerce quotes President Eisenhower as viewing the American success in dealing with the 1953-1954 recession as one attributable to business executives who have become accustomed to thinking in "ambitious long-range terms" and who, expecting the economy to grow and prosper, do not permit minor variations in sales to divert them from their long-range goals.[7]

The Committee for Economic Development finds much merit in holding business responsible for economic stability. This organization is especially concerned with what the individual business can do. In CED terms, "Business does not, cannot, and should not act 'as a whole.' The organization of business into private cartels or government regulated NRA's is inconsistent with the principles of our free economy, even if the stated objective is something as desirable as economic stabilization."[8] Significantly, the Committee's method by which the individual business can make a contribution to stability corresponds closely to the findings of this study: "In part, they [the business units] can . . . [contribute] . . . by doing better the things they already do well—such as developing new products to satisfy new wants, applying improved production methods to reduce costs and bring more products within the reach of more people, and selling constructively . . . In addition they can improve their investment and inventory policy."[9]

Although explicit (and verbal) support for business planning is quite abundant among business leaders and groups, it must be admitted that less support is offered in the writings of economic scholars. However, it is the author's contention that scholastic quiescence in this connection is attributable more to a failure to study the proposal than to a lack of confidence in its potential.

THE PESSIMISTS

Many distinguished scholars have implicitly condemned business planning through their support of government stabilization programs. For the most part, however, the case against business planning has never been clearly stated. It has simply been dismissed without a hearing.

Frequently, those who condemn business planning explicitly do so because they fail to grasp the significance of the proposal as it has been outlined in the preceding pages. The plan is often interpreted as one of counter-cyclical action by individual units. Such a plan, the author would agree, is not deserving of support, primarily because of its extreme reliance upon forecasting devices which in fact do not function adequately. Those not afflicted with the counter-cyclical bent often assume that business planning must be comprehensive industry planning of the Copeland-Ezekiel-Beveridge type or it is not planning at all. David McCord Wright, for example, after giving initial mild support to the type of proposal presented herein slides into a consideration of a method featuring central *ex ante* licensing of various projects.[10] Still another avenue of interpretation is exhibited by Bert G. Hickman, who believes a process of stabilizing the operations of all firms is necessarily involved.[11]

It seems unnecessary to go further into the details of those who are negatively inclined. Criticisms expressed have been mentioned throughout this brief work. A reiteration would only be tedious to the reader. Suffice it to say that critics, by and large, base their cases (if indeed one is judged necessary) on factors not included in the proposal.

THE AUTHOR'S VIEWPOINT

A Statement of Probability. If this study has convinced the reader that business planning cannot be relied upon to produce aggregate economic stability in the United States, the work must be deemed at least a partial success. Clearly, the proposal does not *guarantee* stability. The degree of certainty provided depends upon the actual rationality of the business entities, upon the felt urgency which stability has for each of the firms, and upon the extent of concentration which characterizes the economy.

The Challenge of Inauguration. The business planning proposal presents a formidable challenge to every business unit. Convenient though it is to theorize about non-cyclical motivation, one must surely have some qualms about its realism for the millions of small firms in the present economy. The small scale units have certainly reached the stage of cycle consciousness; whether they are ready to go beyond that to the state of rationality is quite another question and one which a gradual introduction of the plan alone can answer. The gradual introduction, featuring a decreasing degree of government planning, has the added advantage of allowing time for business concentration in those areas characterized by numerous independent units.

The proposal's implied association of rationality with concentration seems valid. The association between size and felt social responsibility too seems true. Indeed, it is because of these associations that the scheme can be viewed with genuine optimism today. Although our present constituents are largely incapable of significant non-cyclical rationality, given education, concentration, and time, that stage can seemingly be reached. Big business, as revealed, already displays to some degree those characteristics which the business stabilization scheme demands. Its influence on the total organization will accelerate the advancement of the as yet irrational units to the basic stages demanded.

Government and Education. Government can promote action in three distinct areas. Education, an inculcation of the fundamental logic of our current institutional system, though the most time consuming and the most difficult to enact, is also the most reliable means to the end. Legislation, easing business concentration, provides a second avenue. The dissemination of economic information provides a third approach. It is in the first and last areas that unique potential lies.

Under business planning it is possible to achieve a very high mean value ratio, and further, to make this ratio approach the stability "success ratio" with a high degree of certainty simply through the education of existing firms. For critics who fear the effects of oligopolistic markets, the business planning proposal allows increased stability assurance under the existing organization simply through increasing the understanding and hence the rationality of the included units. That this process is a slower and more difficult method of achieving a high success probability than is concentration is acknowledged. But, it is nevertheless a possibility which avoids both government planning and increasing bigness in business.

The dissemination of information by government can be expected to have an effect similar in type to education though much smaller in magnitude. If coupled with an education program, the combination may be capable of producing a high "success ratio" without the aid of more concentrated enterprises.

The repeated concern for education in this discussion suggests a need for an intensive study to determine the most appropriate form. Such a determination is beyond the scope of this investigation. Nevertheless, one might surmise that the high schools and universities would bear the burden. At the same time, the power of publicly sponsored training lectures, government "moral suasion" campaigns, and of big business influence ought not to be overlooked.

Conflicting Tendencies of the Proposal and Their Outcomes. As long as rationality must take the form of non-cyclical planning, increased rationality in firm behavior unaccompanied by increased concentration shortens the economic horizon and thus lowers the rationality potential for each member of the group. Increased rationality results in decreased rationality. Increased market knowledge, while extending the economic horizon for one firm, simultaneously limits the horizon of all firms whose actions depend upon that firm.

Fortunately, the significance of this paradox in the application of the plan is much reduced when it is remembered that bigness in business is a fact. Relative giants are already able to act rationally toward economic stability. Thus, the dissemination of market knowledge extends the economic horizon of these units. The probability of "right" action for the large business units is increased and the stability "success ratio" for the economy as a whole is simultaneously augmented. Further, the increased certainty of big business action compensates at least to some degree for the simultaneous loss in economic horizon suffered by small firms facing the uncertainty that surrounds their increasingly rational associates. Consequently, the dissemination of information and the improvement of education are essential factors in even the early transitional stages of the plan.

To concentrate the majority of small business units in the economy in an attempt to gain rational action and higher success probabilities suggests still another conflict. While increasing the mean ratio, concentration, through its decreasing effect on the number of firms, decreases the certainty of the mean ratio equalling the "success ratio" for the economy. Of course, a relatively greater increase in the mean value ratio will more than compensate for the decline in the certainty of the Bernoulli inequality. Yet, to hold that such will always be true is a bold assumption. It would seem wiser to grant that for a high mean value ratio achieved through increased concentration, a price of decreased certainty of this ratio becoming the stability "success ratio" must be paid.

It should be emphasized that the continuing presence of irrational firms in the economy, while lowering the value of the mean ratio does not reduce the certainty of the Bernoulli inequality. The probability of "right" action by the irrational firms may be expected to be low. Nevertheless, the probability of the mean value of such probabilities for all firms being equal to the "success ratio" for the whole economy is unaffected.

At this point, it seems particularly relevant to restate the comment with which this appraisal began. That is, the business planning proposal only provides the circumstances under which aggregate economic stability will *probably* result. The outcome is not assured in any sense. However, nor is it assured under a scheme of industry or government planning unless a most effective single monopoly dominates the scene. In that instance, call it what one wishes, stability can be made certain. But so too, with complete monopoly, can the business plan provide a guarantee.

The Principal Advantage of the Plan. The prime advantage of the plan recommended lies in the fact that it builds upon the American tradition of dispersion, individualism, and private enterprise. Although its certainty of success increases with the increasing concentration of business, the probability of stability also rises with the dissemination of market knowledge and the education of existing firms. Concentration (monopoly) or other form of cooperation (collectivization), though a strong supporting factor, is not a prerequisite for the success of the proposal.

Nor is a prescribed behavior pattern imposed upon any firm or group of firms. Each firm pursues non-cyclical and/or stability oriented objectives as it sees fit. Under these conditions, particularly until firms are much better educated than at present, the probability of realizing stability may be significantly less than it would be under government planning in the same organizational setting. This uncertainty of achievement, if it exists to a greater degree under business planning, is thought to be compensated for by the preservation of business individuality.

Another favorable quality of the business program is that it builds upon the prevailing trends in production. The larger the business units become, the more pervasive the force of automation, and the more effective the planning proposal is likely to be. Moreover, its effectiveness increases irrespective of the pattern of concentration. "Key segments" are of much less import here than in other plans. Concentration in any area, though dispersion remains in others, contributes to a higher stability "success ratio" for the entire economy.

Forecasting lacks are not nearly so limiting in the business plan as would be the case in industry and government schemes. Under business planning, any firm may err in its recognition of consequences ensuing from particular actions. However, the probability that a majority of firms will err in the same direction is small. In the case of industry and government planning, action based on a "right" prediction will lead to a relatively higher probability of stability achievement. At the same time, however, a "wrong" prediction is wrong for all and is equally conducive to a high probability of doom. Forecasting being as precarious as it is, the business scheme must consequently be held desirable on still another count.

Inherent Limitations of the Plan. The many advantages of the business proposal must not be allowed to overshadow its potential weaknesses. A principal defect seems to lie in the dependence upon individual firm rationality and social responsibility. In the case of large business units, it seems probable that firms will behave in the manner demanded. However, in the case of small independent units, traditionally irrational and equipped with only a short economic horizon, the behavior may not fit the expectations of the business planners. That education can insure rational action and social responsibility may be claimed. Nevertheless, the probability of achieving stability may be so low during the training interval as to make the plan impractical. An increase in business concentration sufficient to offset the low probabilities of "right" actions of small firms might then be a necessary step if the plan is to succeed. If so, the meritorious qualities of dispersion and individuality lose much of their luster.

Although not a weakness in the proposal, the law of large numbers must be treated with caution. It should not be interpreted as making something out of nothing; it does not generate stability from any actions of firms. The law of large numbers builds upon the probabilities of "right" action alone. From the probability of individual firms acting in a manner favorable to stability, the law indicates that there is a resulting probability of aggregate stability achievement. And the higher the probability of "right" action for the individual firm, the higher the "success ratio" for the economy as a whole. But, if firms are irrational and victims of erroneous forecasting, the elemental probability values decline and the probability of aggregate success similarly declines. To reiterate once more, the business planning proposal rests upon the rationality of individual, independent business entities and not upon the magic of any mathematical law.

Conclusion. One's final appraisal of the business planning proposal hinges upon one's sense of values, especially as it concerns dispersion of control, individuality, and private initiative. To those sympathetic to these qualities, a somewhat uncertain stability can be provided by the immediate inauguration of the business plan. To those more inclined toward security, concentration can give the business proposal a stability potential of any certainty desired. To those with patience, education can make the proposal yield a rather certain stability without infringing further upon individuality and initiative through increased concentration. The business planning proposal is flexible, practical, and to most American businessmen, appealing. Its potential depends wholly upon the comfort with which individual business units wear the double harness of social responsibility and rationality.

REFERENCES

CHAPTER I

[1] Morris A. Copeland, "Business Stabilization by Agreement," *American Economic Review*, XXXIV (1944), pp. 328-340; Mordecai Ezekiel, *Jobs for All* (New York, Knopf, 1939), 298 pp.

[2] Edward C. Simmons, quoted in: *Monetary, Credit and Fiscal Policies* (Washington, Joint Committee of the Economic Report, 1949), p. 398.

[3] "Business-and-Government," *Fortune*, XVII (June, 1938), p. 52.

[4] "Whistling in the Economic Dark," *Fortune*, XLVIII (November, 1953), p. 111.

[5] *Ibid.*, p. 112.

[6] "The Type of Business Men We Need," *The Calgary* (Canada) *Herald*, April 25, 1955, p. 4.

[7] *Ibid.*

[8] Herrymon Maurer, "The Age of Managers," *Fortune*, LI (January, 1955), p. 86.

[9] "Whistling in the Economic Dark," p. 112.

[10] *The Full Employment Act of 1945*, Hearings Before a Subcommittee of the Committee on Banking and Currency, United States Senate, 79th Congress, 1st Session, Senate Document 380 (Washington, 1945), p. 463.

[11] *Wall Street Journal*, April 4, 1955, p. 1.

[12] Joseph E. Evans, "Guaranteed Change," *Wall Street Journal*, April 21, 1955, p. 10.

[13] *Employment Stabilization* (New York, National Association of Manufacturers, 1952), p. 3.

[14] *Ibid.*, p. 4.

[15] Walter P. Egle, *Economic Stabilization* (Princeton, Princeton University Press, 1952), p. 186.

[16] Wesley C. Mitchell, *Business Cycles: The Problem and Its Setting* (New York, National Bureau of Economic Research, 1927), p. 156.

[17] Hans F. Sennholz, *How Can Europe Survive?* (New York, Van Nostrand, 1955), p. 24.

[18] Elmer C. Bratt, *Business Cycles and Forecasting* (Homewood, Ill., Irwin, 1953), p. 511.

[19] Dexter M. Keezer, *Making Capitalism Work* (New York, McGraw-Hill, 1950), p. 59.

CHAPTER II

[1] D. H. Robertson, *Banking Policy and the Price Level* (London, Staples Press, 1926), Ch. 2.

[2] Alvin H. Hansen, *Economic Stabilization in an Unbalanced World* (New York, Harcourt, Brace, 1932), pp. 192-193.

[3] D. H. Robertson, p. 94; James A. Estey, *Business Cycles* (New York, Prentice-Hall, 1950), p. 163.

[4] Karl Mannheim, *Freedom, Power, and Democratic Planning* (New York, Oxford University Press, 1950), p. 303.

[5] Stephen K. Bailey, "Political Elements in Full Employment Policy," *American Economic Review*, XLV (1955), p. 342.

[6] The adjectives "elemental," "atomistic," "individual," and "micro" are used synonymously to refer to characteristics of components rather than of wholes.

CHAPTER III

[1] F. A. Hayek, "The Use of Knowledge in Society," *American Economic Review*, XXXV (1945), p. 524.

[2] Frank H. Knight, *Risk, Uncertainty and Profit* (New York, Houghton-Mifflin, 1921), p. 268.

[3] Joan Robinson, "Imperfect Competition Revisited," *Economic Journal*, LXII (1953), p. 582.

[4] John R. Commons, *Legal Foundations of Capitalism* (New York, Macmillan, 1924), p. 145.

[5] Sidney Schoeffler, "Toward a General Definition of Rational Action," *Kyklos*, VII (1954), pp. 270-271.

[6] The "dual-morality of man" concept (Chapter II) is again suggested. That there may be conflict between individual and social interests in both the short and the long run is not denied. Yet it is maintained that the businessman will be socially responsible to the degree that he will modify his actions to benefit both *himself and society whenever possible.* It is not demanded that he sacrifice his own welfare for stability's sake. Indeed, that he need not do so will be shown in a subsequent section.

[7] See, for example, the testimony of: Fritz Machlup, "Marginal Analysis and Empirical Research," *American Economic Review*, XXXVI (1946), p. 520; William Graham Sumner, *Folkways* (Boston, Ginn, 1902), p. 2; F. A. Hayek, *Road to Serfdom* (Chicago, University of Chicago Press, 1944), p. 164; Joseph A. Schumpeter, *The Theory of Econimic Development* (Cambridge, Harvard University Press, 1934), p. 91.

[8] If M is the set of possible consequences that may be expected to arise from any particular action, and further, if x denotes any one of these consequences, x is a *variable* in M. In addition, z is a *continuous variable* if for every consequence z_0 there exists another consequence z_1 in M only slightly different from z_0.

[9] G. L. S. Shackle, *Expectations in Economics* (London, Cambridge Unversity Press, 1949), p. 22.

[10] Herbert A. Simon, *Administrative Behavior* (New York, Macmillan, 1954), p. 79.

[11] William Fellner, *Monetary Policies and Full Employment* (Berkeley, University of California Press, 1946), p. 154.

[12] George J. Stigler, *The Theory of Competitive Price* (New York, Macmillan, 1952), p. 96.

[13] Louis Baudin, "Irrationality in Economics," *Quarterly Journal of Economics*, LXVIII (1954), p. 487.

[14] John Maynard Keynes, *The General Theory of Employment, Interest and Money* (London, Macmillan, 1936), p. 152.

[15] William Fellner, p. 154.

[16] George Katona, "Psychological Analysis of Business Decisions," *American Economic Review*, XXXVI (1946), pp. 61-62.

[17] Albert G. Hart, "Liquidity and Uncertainty," *American Economic Review*, XXXIX (1949), p. 180.
A 45-1 long-shot certain to lose would attract no customers to the Ten-Dollar-Win

wicket; only because there is uncertainty concerning the outcome of the race is there a demand for betting tickets on such an entry.

[18] Jakob Marschak, "Lack of Confidence," *Social Research*, VIII (1941), p. 51.

[19] John Maynard Keynes, p. 161.

[20] Gerhard Colm, "Fiscal Policy," *The New Economics* (New York, Knopf, 1948), p. 461.

[21] Baudin, p. 494.

[22] George Katona and James N. Morgan, "The Quantitative Study of Factors Determining Business Decisions," *Quarterly Jorunal of Economics*, LXVI (1952), p. 84.

[23] Arthur C. Pigou, *Industrial Fluctuations* (London, Macmillan, 1937), p. 27.

[24] Alexander Leighton, cited in: Stuart Chase et al, *The Social Responsibility of Management* (New York, New York University, 1951), p. 18.

[25] Armen A. Alchian, "Uncertainty, Evolution, and Economic Theory," *Journal of Political Economy*, LVIII (1950), p. 212; Gerard Tintner, "Theory of Choice Under Subjective Risk and Uncertainty," *Econometrica*, IX (1941), pp. 298-304.

[26] A single-valued function is one such that for every independent variable (the determining event), there corresponds only one dependent variable (the determined outcome). In other words, the consequence of an action is certain and is not subject to a range of outcomes.

[27] Andrea P. Papandreou, "Some Basic Problems in the Theory of the Firm," *A Survey of Contemporary Economics* (Homewood, Irwin, 1952), p. 208.

CHAPTER IV

[1] Irwin Friend, "What Business Can Do To Prevent Recession," *Problems in Anti-Recession Policy* (New York, Committee for Economic Development, 1954), p. 3. Friend states that currently about one-half of the largest non-financial corporations (those in the top one hundred) have capital budgets extending three years into the future.

[2] Joel Dean, "The Concept and Economic Significance of Regularization of Business Investment," *Regularization of Business Investment* (Princeton, Princeton University Press, 1954), p. 60.

[3] Clarence B. Randall, *Good News About Jobs* (New York, National Association of Manufacturers, 1946).

[4] Melvin G. De Chazeau, "Business Investment Policies," *Problems in Anti-Recession Policy*, p. 17.

[5] Reducable uncertainty, as opposed to what has earlier been termed true uncertainty, may be transformed into a probability coefficient and allowed for. This allowance is here termed a risk premium.

[6] For a review of the evidence on this matter, see: Irwin Friend and Jean Bronfenbrenner, "Business Investment Programs and their Realization," *Survey of Current Business* (Washington, Department of Commerce, 1950), pp. 11-22; "Plant and Equipment Programs and their Realization," *Short-Term Economic Forecasting* (Princeton, Princeton University Press, 1955), pp. 53-112; Ira Mosher, cited in: *The Full Employment Act of 1945*, p. 469; Franco Modigliani, et al, "Economic Expectations and Plans of Firms in Relation to Short-Term Forecasting," *Short-Term Economic Forecasting*, p. 278; Robert Ferber, "On the Accuracy of Businessmen's Expectations," *Current Economic Comment*, XVI (May, 1954), pp. 3-12.

[7] Kenneth E. Boulding, *The Economics of Peace* (New York, Prentice-Hall, 1945), pp. 137-138.

[8] Benjamin Caplan, "Comment: Recent Developments in Short-Term Forecasting," *Short-Term Economic Forecasting*, p. 43.

[9] John H. G. Pierson, "Facts, Issues and Policies," *American Economic Review*, XXXVI (1946), p. 319.

[10] Joseph A. Schumpeter, *Capitalism, Socialism, and Democracy* (New York, Harper, 1942), p. 84.

[11] Paul G. Hoffman, cited in: Emerson P. Schmidt, "Promoting Steadier Output and Sales," *Regularization of Business Investment*, p. 353.

[12] Howard R. Bowen, "Technological Change and Aggregate Demand," *American Economic Review*, XLIV (1954), pp. 917-921.

[13] "Technical superiority in production" is a relative measure of one firm's ability to compete by virtue of its productive technique with other firms within a given industry or even with outher industries. The cost function is a dominant element in this measure; elements of product appeal, production and marketing flexibility, and public relations are other factors.

[14] Melvin G. De Chazeau, p. 17.

[15] One of the best statements on this subject is to be found in *Automation: A New Dimension to Old Problems* by George Shultz and George Baldwin (Washington, D. C., Public Affairs Press, 1955).

[16] Nathan Belfer, "A Theory of the Automatic Reabsorption of Technologically Displaced Labor," *Southern Economic Journal*, XVI (1949), p. 36.

[17] Walter S. Buckingham, quoted in: "Automation and the Labor Force," *Business and Economic Conditions* (February, 1956), p. 22.

[18] Melvin G. De Chazeau, p. 20.

CHAPTER V

[1] E. A. G. Robinson, *Monopoly* (Cambridge, Cambridge University Press, 1949), p. 49.

[2] Joan Robinson, p. 583.

[3] Thorstein Veblen, *The Theory of Business Enterprise* (New York, Scribner's, 1904), pp. 45-48.

[4] Edward H. Chamberlin, "Monopolistic Competition Revisited," *Economica*, XVIII (1951), p. 357.

[5] Joan Robinson, p. 583.

[6] Edward H. Chamberlin, *The Theory of Monopolistic Competition* (Cambridge, Harvard University Press, 1933), p. 53.

CHAPPTER VI

[1] Alvin H. Hansen, *Monetary Theory and Fiscal Policy* (New York, McGraw-Hill, 1949), p. 198.

[2] John K. Galbraith, *American Capitalism: The Concept of Countervailing Power* (Boston, Houghton-Mifflin, 1952), p. 58.

[3] Robert A. Brady, *Business as a System of Power* (New York, Columbia University Press, 1943), p. 14.

[4] John K. Galbraith, p. 116.

[5] Joseph A. Schumpeter, p. 84.

[6] *Ibid.*

[7] Wesley C. Mitchell, *The Backward Art of Spending Money* (New York, McGraw-Hill, 1937), p. 338.

CHAPTER VII

[1] Walter P. Egle, pp. 98-106.

[2] Edgar M. Hoover, "Cyclical Behavior of Investment: Comment," *Regularization of Business Investment*, p. 69.

[3] Joel Dean, p. 63.

[4] David McCord Wright, "The Concept and Significance of Regularization of Business Investment," *Regularization of Business Investment*, p. 71.

[5] Irwin Friend, p. 1; A. D. H. Kaplan, *The Guarantee of Annual Wages* (Washington, Brookings, 1947), p. 168.

[6] Harlow H. Curtice, *Facing the Future with Confidence* (Detroit, General Motors Corporation, 1955).

[7] *Can We Depression Proof Our Economy?* (Washington, United States Chamber of Commerce, 1955), p. 6.

[8] *Defense Against Recession: Policy for Greater Economic Stability* (New York, Committee for Economic Development, 1954), pp. 15-16.

[9] *Ibid.*

[10] David McCord Wright, p. 71.

[11] Bert G. Hickman, "Cyclical Behavior of Investment: Comment," *Regularization of Business Investment*, pp. 35-37.

ABOUT THE AUTHOR

A native of Calgary, Henry Thomassen attended universities in both Canada and the United States. In 1956 he received the Ph.D. degree in economics at the University of Nebraska. His experiences have varied from elementary school teaching to service as an officer with the Royal Canadian Army. During 1956-57, he was a member of the faculty of Georgia State College. In addition to a monograph, *Trends in Economic Education*, published by Public Affairs Press in 1956, he has published articles in leading professional economics and education journals. Currently, he is an economist for the Prudential Insurance Company of America in Newark, New Jersey.